Web Development with PHP: Build Dynamic Websites from Scratch

A Step-by-Step Guide to Developing Web Apps with PHP

BOOZMAN RICHARD

BOOKER BLUNT

Table of Content

TABLE OF CONTENTS

INTRODUCTION

Web Development with PHP: Build Dynamic Websites from Scratch

In today's rapidly evolving digital landscape, the need for dynamic, interactive, and scalable web applications has never been greater. As businesses and individuals continue to rely on the internet to connect with customers, manage content, and provide services, web development remains at the heart of the modern technological ecosystem. Among the many programming languages available for web development, **PHP** (Hypertext Preprocessor) stands out as one of the most versatile, reliable, and widely used languages.

This book, **"Web Development with PHP: Build Dynamic Websites from Scratch,"** is designed to equip you with the knowledge, tools, and techniques to harness the power of PHP and create modern, high-performance web applications. Whether you're a beginner just starting out or an experienced developer looking to deepen your PHP expertise, this comprehensive guide will walk you through every step of the web development process—from the fundamentals of PHP to advanced concepts like building

RESTful APIs, integrating databases, and deploying scalable applications.

Why PHP?

PHP has been around for over two decades and is still one of the most commonly used programming languages for server-side web development. Its flexibility, simplicity, and ease of integration with databases make it an excellent choice for building dynamic websites and web applications. From personal blogs to enterprise-level platforms, PHP powers millions of websites worldwide. Its popularity is partly due to its rich ecosystem of frameworks, tools, and libraries, which greatly accelerate development, allowing developers to focus on building unique features instead of reinventing the wheel.

PHP's ability to work seamlessly with **MySQL**, **PostgreSQL**, and **SQLite** databases, along with its integration with frontend technologies such as HTML, CSS, and JavaScript, makes it an ideal language for creating dynamic web pages and applications that interact with users in real-time. Additionally, PHP frameworks like **Laravel**, **Symfony**, and **CodeIgniter** further enhance its capabilities, enabling developers to build scalable, maintainable, and secure applications more efficiently.

What Will You Learn from This Book?

This book is carefully structured to provide a comprehensive and hands-on approach to learning PHP for web development. It covers everything from the basics to advanced topics, ensuring that you not only gain a deep understanding of PHP itself but also acquire the skills to create fully functional and secure web applications.

The key areas that this book will guide you through include:

1. **PHP Fundamentals**: You'll begin by learning the basics of PHP, including syntax, data types, operators, and control structures. You'll get comfortable with writing PHP scripts that interact with users, handle forms, and perform basic data operations.

2. **Database Integration**: A significant portion of modern web development revolves around databases, and this book will teach you how to connect your PHP application to a database using **MySQL**. You'll learn how to perform CRUD

9

operations (Create, Read, Update, Delete) and understand how to design and structure your database for optimal performance.

3. **Building RESTful APIs**: As web applications become more interconnected, understanding how to build **RESTful APIs** is a crucial skill for modern PHP developers. This book will guide you through the process of creating a secure, efficient, and scalable API that can serve as the backbone for mobile apps, client-side frameworks (such as React or Vue), or third-party services.

4. **Working with PHP Frameworks**: Learn how to use powerful PHP frameworks like **Laravel** to streamline development and make your applications more maintainable. You'll understand the principles behind **MVC architecture**, routing, controllers, and views, and you'll gain experience building real-world projects.

5. **Security Best Practices**: Security is paramount in web development, and this book will teach you how to safeguard your applications against common web vulnerabilities like **SQL injection, cross-site scripting (XSS)**, and **cross-site request forgery (CSRF)**. You'll also learn about **password hashing,**

sessions, and **cookies** to ensure that your users' data remains secure.

6. **Performance Optimization**: As your web applications grow, performance becomes a critical concern. This book will cover best practices for optimizing your PHP applications, including techniques like **caching, query optimization**, and **using tools like Xdebug** for profiling and debugging your code.

7. **Deploying PHP Applications**: Once you've built your PHP application, this book will guide you through the deployment process. You'll learn how to set up a production environment, transfer files securely using FTP/SFTP, and set up **version control with Git** to streamline your development process.

Who This Book is For

This book is designed for a broad audience, including:

- **Beginners**: If you're new to web development and PHP, this book will take you step by step through the process of learning the language and building your first web applications.

11

- **Intermediate Developers**: If you already have some experience with PHP or web development, this book will help you deepen your knowledge and learn best practices, advanced techniques, and modern tools used in PHP development.

- **Experienced Developers**: Even experienced developers will find value in this book as it covers new and advanced features in PHP, including **PHP 8** and **modern frameworks** like **Laravel**. You'll also gain insights into best practices for secure, scalable, and efficient application design.

A Hands-On Approach

Throughout this book, you'll be guided by **hands-on examples** and **practical projects**. Each chapter includes code snippets, explanations, and exercises that you can implement on your own to reinforce your learning. By the end of this book, you will have the knowledge to build fully functional PHP-based web applications—from simple blogs to complex, database-driven platforms.

The goal is to ensure that you are not only learning PHP syntax but also understanding the underlying concepts and how to apply them to real-world projects. The book's practical approach will ensure that you have the skills to start developing your own projects right away.

Why Learn PHP?

As one of the most widely used programming languages for web development, **PHP** continues to evolve with modern features and practices that make it more powerful, efficient, and secure than ever before. Learning PHP opens up a wide range of opportunities, from building personal websites to developing enterprise-level applications. PHP also integrates seamlessly with modern tools and technologies, including front-end frameworks, databases, and cloud-based services, making it an essential skill for any web developer.

This book will not only teach you PHP but also prepare you for the future of web development, equipping you with the skills needed to build dynamic, scalable, and secure web applications. Whether you're looking to enhance your career as a web developer, build your own projects, or dive into the world of **backend development**, this book is your comprehensive guide to mastering PHP.

Conclusion

In this book, we aim to provide you with a thorough and hands-on understanding of PHP and its role in web development. By learning PHP, you'll gain a powerful tool that powers some of the most popular websites and applications in the world. With PHP, the possibilities are endless, and this book will ensure that you have a solid foundation for building robust, dynamic web applications.

Let's dive in and start building your first PHP-powered website!

CHAPTER 1

INTRODUCTION TO PHP AND WEB DEVELOPMENT

What is PHP?

PHP, which stands for **Hypertext Preprocessor**, is a widely used open-source scripting language primarily designed for web development. Initially created by **Rasmus Lerdorf** in 1994, PHP has evolved to become one of the most popular server-side programming languages. It is especially well-suited for creating dynamic and interactive websites.

Unlike client-side languages like JavaScript, which run in the user's browser, PHP runs on the **server**, meaning it is responsible for generating the content that gets displayed on a web page. PHP interacts with databases, processes user input, and dynamically generates HTML content to be displayed on a user's browser.

PHP code is embedded within HTML files using `<?php ?>` tags, which allows for seamless integration of static and dynamic content. Whether you're creating a simple website or a complex web application, PHP offers a vast range of functions and libraries to simplify your tasks. It can handle everything from form submission and user authentication to complex database queries.

15

The Role of PHP in Web Development

PHP plays a central role in **server-side web development**. It acts as the backbone of many websites, enabling them to serve dynamic content that can change based on user interaction, preferences, or time of day. Here's a closer look at how PHP fits into the broader scope of web development:

1. **Dynamic Content Generation**: PHP is commonly used to generate HTML dynamically based on the input from users or the content in a database. For example, when a user logs into a website, PHP can check the credentials stored in a database and display personalized content based on the user's role.

2. **Form Handling**: Many web applications involve form submissions (like login forms, contact forms, or search forms). PHP processes these forms on the server, validating and storing the data, or responding to the user with appropriate feedback.

3. **Database Interaction**: PHP works seamlessly with databases like MySQL, allowing web developers to perform operations such as reading, writing, updating, and deleting data. This interaction is essential for any website that relies on dynamic content, such as e-commerce sites or content management systems (CMS) like WordPress.

16

4. **User Authentication**: PHP can handle user login systems, managing sessions and cookies to ensure users are authenticated and their information is kept secure during their interaction with the website.

5. **Handling Files**: PHP also helps manage files on the server, such as uploading images or documents, or creating and managing directories.

Overall, PHP's versatility and robustness make it an indispensable tool for web developers. It integrates easily with many other technologies, which is why it remains one of the most used programming languages for server-side development.

PHP vs. Other Web Technologies

PHP often competes with other server-side technologies like **JavaScript (Node.js)**, **Python (Django/Flask)**, **Ruby (Ruby on Rails)**, and **Java (Spring)**. Here's how PHP compares to some of these technologies:

1. **PHP vs. JavaScript (Node.js)**:
   o PHP is primarily used for server-side scripting, while JavaScript, with the help of **Node.js**, enables full-stack development (both client and server-side).
   o JavaScript can execute on both the client and server, making it a more versatile language for

17

full-stack development. In contrast, PHP is strictly for server-side operations.

- o PHP's syntax is easier for beginners and widely adopted for legacy systems, while JavaScript (Node.js) allows for more real-time, event-driven applications.

2. **PHP vs. Python**:

- o Python frameworks like **Django** and **Flask** have gained popularity for their simplicity and readability. However, PHP has been the standard for web development for many years, with tools like **Laravel** offering modern PHP frameworks that rival Django in functionality.
- o Python is used for a wider range of applications (including data science and machine learning), while PHP is strictly focused on web development.
- o PHP's ecosystem is deeply integrated with web hosting environments, while Python might require additional configuration for deployment on web servers.

3. **PHP vs. Ruby**:

- o **Ruby on Rails**, a full-stack web framework, is similar to PHP frameworks like **Laravel**. Ruby has a reputation for elegant syntax, while PHP is often regarded as more straightforward.

18

- o PHP is more widely supported by web hosts and has a larger community and older projects than Ruby, which might have fewer legacy applications.

4. **PHP vs. Java**:
   - o Java is often used in large-scale enterprise applications and is known for its performance and scalability. PHP is more suited to small and medium-scale web applications, though with frameworks like **Laravel** and **Symfony**, PHP can handle enterprise-level systems as well.
   - o Java applications require more complex setups (e.g., Java Virtual Machine), whereas PHP is simpler and faster to deploy.

In summary, PHP is a solid choice for building web applications and is often preferred due to its simplicity, widespread use, and robust ecosystem of frameworks. While other languages may be better suited for certain types of applications, PHP remains a go-to option for web development.

Setting Up Your Development Environment (Installing PHP, IDEs, and Server Setup)

Before diving into PHP development, it's essential to set up your local development environment. Here's a step-by-step guide to getting started with PHP development:

1. **Installing PHP**:

    o   On **Windows**, the easiest way to install PHP is by using a package like **XAMPP** or **WAMP**, which provides Apache, MySQL, and PHP all bundled together.

    o   On **Mac**, you can use **MAMP** or install PHP directly via **Homebrew**. Alternatively, you can set up a LAMP stack (Linux, Apache, MySQL, PHP) if you're on Linux.

    o   To install PHP manually, visit the official PHP download page and follow the installation instructions for your operating system.

2. **Setting up a Web Server**: PHP requires a web server to run. If you're using a package like XAMPP or MAMP, the server is already set up for you. Otherwise, you'll need to install **Apache** or **Nginx** and configure it to handle PHP scripts. You'll also need to configure the server to point to the folder where your PHP files are stored.

3. **Installing a Database (MySQL)**:

    o   For dynamic applications, you'll need a database like MySQL to store and retrieve data. Most PHP setups, such as XAMPP or MAMP, come with MySQL pre-installed. Alternatively, you can install MySQL separately.

    o   Once MySQL is installed, use **phpMyAdmin** (a web-based interface for managing MySQL databases) or command-line tools to create and manage your databases.

4. **Choosing an Integrated Development Environment (IDE)**:

   o An IDE can help make PHP development easier by providing syntax highlighting, code completion, and debugging tools.

   o Popular IDEs for PHP development include:

      ▪ **PHPStorm**: A powerful, feature-rich IDE specifically designed for PHP.

      ▪ **Visual Studio Code (VSCode)**: A lightweight, free editor with excellent PHP support via extensions.

      ▪ **NetBeans**: A free, open-source IDE with built-in support for PHP.

      ▪ **Sublime Text**: A fast, flexible text editor that can be enhanced with plugins for PHP development.

5. **Configuring Your Local Environment**: After installing PHP and a web server, configure your **php.ini** file (found in the PHP installation directory). This file allows you to modify settings such as:

   o **Error Reporting**: Enable error reporting to see helpful debugging messages.

   o **Max File Upload Size**: If you're working with file uploads, adjust the file size limits in php.ini.

21

    o **Timezone Settings**: Make sure PHP is set to use the correct timezone for your location.

6. **Testing Your Setup**: Once everything is installed and configured, create a test PHP file, like `info.php`, with the following code:

```php
php
```

```php
<?php
phpinfo();
?>
```

This will output detailed information about your PHP installation and server configuration, allowing you to confirm that everything is working correctly.

By the end of this chapter, you should be able to:

- Understand what PHP is and its role in web development.
- Compare PHP with other web technologies.
- Set up a local development environment with PHP, MySQL, and a web server.
- Choose and configure an IDE that suits your development style.

This setup will allow you to begin building dynamic websites and applications with PHP, providing the foundation for the rest of your PHP web development journey.

CHAPTER 2

UNDERSTANDING THE BASICS OF WEB DEVELOPMENT

Client-side vs. Server-side Development

Understanding the distinction between **client-side** and **server-side** development is crucial in web development, as both play integral roles in delivering dynamic and interactive websites.

1. **Client-side Development**:
    - **What It Is**: Client-side development refers to the operations and technologies that occur in the user's web browser. When a user visits a website, their browser downloads files (HTML, CSS, JavaScript) and displays them to the user. The client-side handles the presentation and user interaction.
    - **Technologies Involved**: The main technologies used in client-side development are:
        - **HTML (HyperText Markup Language)**: Defines the structure of the web page (headings, paragraphs, images, etc.).

23

- **CSS (Cascading Style Sheets)**: Defines the visual presentation, such as colors, fonts, layouts, and responsiveness.
- **JavaScript**: Adds interactivity and behavior to the webpage (form validation, animations, dynamic content changes).

○ **Examples**:

- **HTML**: Basic page structure like headings, links, and paragraphs.
- **CSS**: Styling elements to make the page visually appealing (e.g., changing text color or layout).
- **JavaScript**: Interactivity like dropdown menus, form validation, or fetching data dynamically via AJAX.

○ **Role**: Client-side development focuses on what the user can see and interact with in their browser. It's all about creating an engaging, responsive, and user-friendly experience.

2. **Server-side Development**:

○ **What It Is**: Server-side development refers to the operations that happen on the web server. The server is responsible for processing requests from users, retrieving data, and sending back the appropriate response (e.g., a webpage or an API response).

- o **Technologies Involved**: Server-side development involves server-side programming languages like PHP, Python, Java, Ruby, and Node.js. It may also require a database to store and retrieve data.
- o **Examples**:
  - **PHP**: Generating dynamic HTML pages based on database queries.
  - **Node.js**: Handling HTTP requests and sending dynamic responses.
- o **Role**: Server-side development is essential for processing data, interacting with databases, managing sessions, and ensuring the server handles requests efficiently. The server sends the correct data to the client-side, where it is rendered for the user to interact with.

Client-side vs. Server-side Summary:

- **Client-side**: Focuses on the user interface and experience. Technologies include HTML, CSS, and JavaScript.
- **Server-side**: Focuses on data processing, storage, and application logic. Technologies include PHP, databases, and server-side scripting.

25

Both client-side and server-side development work together to create a fully functional web application. While the client-side provides the look and feel, the server-side powers the backend logic and data handling.

Overview of HTML, CSS, and JavaScript

These three technologies are the cornerstone of modern web development. While **PHP** plays a crucial role in server-side processing, **HTML**, **CSS**, and **JavaScript** are responsible for how content is structured, styled, and made interactive on the client-side.

1. **HTML (HyperText Markup Language)**:
   - **Purpose**: HTML is the backbone of any website. It provides the structure of the web page, defining headings, paragraphs, lists, links, forms, and other elements. It's a markup language used to create the content and layout of the web page.
   - **Elements**: HTML consists of elements represented by **tags**. For example:
     - `<h1>Welcome to My Website</h1>`: Defines a top-level heading.
     - `<p>This is a paragraph.</p>`: Defines a paragraph of text.

26

- <a
  href="https://example.com">Vi
  sit Example</a>: Defines a
  hyperlink.

  o **Key Role in Web Development**: HTML
  provides the skeleton of the webpage, while CSS
  and JavaScript make it look good and interactive.
  Without HTML, a webpage wouldn't have any
  content.

2. **CSS (Cascading Style Sheets)**:

   o **Purpose**: CSS is used to control the presentation
   (layout, colors, fonts, etc.) of the HTML content.
   While HTML provides structure, CSS defines the
   visual appearance.

   o **Selectors and Rules**: CSS works by defining
   selectors (e.g., .container, #header, h1) and
   applying styles to them (e.g., color: blue;,
   font-size: 16px;).

   o **Responsive Design**: CSS can also be used to
   create responsive web designs that adjust based
   on the device's screen size, ensuring a good user
   experience on both desktop and mobile.

   o **Key Role in Web Development**: CSS turns an
   otherwise plain, unstyled HTML page into
   something visually appealing. It enhances the

27

look and feel of the page, making it more engaging and user-friendly.

3. **JavaScript**:

   o **Purpose**: JavaScript is the programming language used to add **interactivity** to web pages. Unlike HTML and CSS, which define the structure and style of a page, JavaScript makes the page dynamic by responding to user actions, like clicks or form submissions.

   o **Interactivity**: JavaScript allows you to:

      ▪ Validate user input in forms before submission.

      ▪ Create dynamic elements like sliders, carousels, and modals.

      ▪ Update content without refreshing the page (using AJAX).

   o **Key Role in Web Development**: JavaScript is essential for creating dynamic and interactive user interfaces. It makes websites feel more responsive and allows for real-time data fetching and user interaction.

How They Work Together:

- **HTML** structures the content.
- **CSS** styles the content.
- **JavaScript** makes the content interactive and dynamic.

28

These three technologies complement each other to create modern, interactive, and engaging websites and web applications. While PHP handles the server-side processing, HTML, CSS, and JavaScript focus on creating a seamless user experience.

Introduction to Databases and the Role of PHP in Backend Development

Databases are a crucial part of web development because they store, retrieve, and manage the data that powers dynamic websites. Web applications often require databases to keep track of information such as user profiles, blog posts, product inventories, and much more.

1. **What is a Database?**

    o A **database** is an organized collection of data that can be accessed, managed, and updated easily. Databases are designed to handle large amounts of information, store data efficiently, and allow for complex queries.

    o **Relational Databases (RDBMS)**: Most web applications use relational databases like **MySQL** or **PostgreSQL**. These databases store data in **tables**, which consist of rows and columns. Each table has a specific purpose, and

29

the data is structured in a way that allows for efficient querying and retrieval.

2. **PHP's Role in Backend Development**:

   o **Connecting to Databases**: PHP can connect to a database (like MySQL) using built-in functions like `mysqli_connect()` or `PDO` (PHP Data Objects). Once connected, PHP can interact with the database to retrieve, insert, update, or delete data.

   o **Executing SQL Queries**: PHP can execute SQL queries to retrieve or modify data. For example, you can use PHP to run a query like:

```php

$result = mysqli_query($conn, "SELECT * FROM users");

```

   This would retrieve all records from the `users` table and display them on the web page.

   o **Managing Data**: PHP handles various tasks related to data management, such as form submissions (e.g., storing user data), content management (e.g., displaying blog posts), and user authentication (e.g., checking usernames and passwords).

3. **How PHP and Databases Work Together**:

- o **Data Storage**: PHP can store and retrieve data from a database. For example, when a user submits a registration form, PHP can take the form data and insert it into a database.
- o **Dynamic Content**: PHP can query the database to display dynamic content on a website. For example, a product page on an e-commerce site can use PHP to pull product details from a database and display them on the webpage.
- o **CRUD Operations**: The four main operations in database management—**Create**, **Read**, **Update**, and **Delete**—are the foundation of how PHP interacts with a database.

PHP and Databases Summary:

- PHP allows you to connect to a database and perform CRUD operations.
- Databases store the data that powers dynamic web applications.
- PHP helps retrieve and display this data in response to user actions, making websites interactive and personalized.

By the end of this chapter, you should have a solid understanding of the basics of web development, the roles of client-side and server-side technologies, the key components of HTML, CSS, and JavaScript, and how PHP interacts with databases in backend development. This foundational knowledge sets the stage for more advanced PHP concepts in the following chapters.

CHAPTER 3

SETTING UP YOUR FIRST PHP SCRIPT

Writing and Running Your First PHP Script

In this section, we'll walk through the steps to write and run your very first PHP script. PHP scripts are embedded within HTML pages, and the server processes them before sending the resulting HTML to the client's browser.

1. **Creating a PHP Script**:

    o Open a text editor or IDE of your choice (e.g., Visual Studio Code, Sublime Text, PHPStorm).

    o Create a new file and save it with a `.php` extension. For example, `firstscript.php`.

    o In the file, write the following code:

    ```
    php
    ```

    ```php
    <?php
        echo "Hello, World!";
    ?>
    ```

    o The `<?php ... ?>` tags are used to denote PHP code. Inside these tags, we've written a PHP

33

function called `echo` that outputs text to the browser.

2. **Running the PHP Script**:

   o **Locally**: If you're working on your local machine, you'll need a web server like Apache (provided by XAMPP or MAMP) to run PHP scripts.

      ▪ Place the PHP file in the **htdocs** folder (for XAMPP) or the **www** folder (for MAMP).

      ▪ Open your web browser and type `http://localhost/firstscript.php`.

      ▪ You should see the message "Hello, World!" displayed in your browser.

   o **On a Remote Server**: Upload your PHP file to a server using FTP or a file manager provided by your web host. Once uploaded, you can access the script using the server's URL (e.g., `http://yourdomain.com/firstscript.php`).

Congratulations! You've just written and run your first PHP script, and now you're ready to dive deeper into PHP syntax and structure.

PHP Syntax and Basic Structure

Understanding PHP syntax is essential for writing effective PHP code. PHP code is embedded within HTML files, and the server processes it to generate the final output.

1. **PHP Tags**:

    o PHP scripts begin with the `<?php` tag and end with the `?>` tag. Everything in between is treated as PHP code. The closing `?>` tag is optional if the PHP script is the last content in the file.

    Example:

    ```php
    php

    <?php
        // PHP code goes here
    ?>
    ```

2. **Comments**:

    o Comments are used to explain the code or mark sections for future reference. They are ignored by the PHP interpreter and do not affect the code execution.

    o **Single-line comment**: Uses `//` for a single line comment.

o **Multi-line comment**: Uses /* to start and */ to end a multi-line comment.

Example:

```php
// This is a single-line comment
/* This is
   a multi-line comment */
```

3. **Case Sensitivity**:

o PHP keywords (such as echo, if, else) are **not case-sensitive**. However, variable names in PHP are case-sensitive.

Example:

```php
$var = "Hello";  // $var
$Var = "World";  // $Var
echo $var;  // Will output: Hello
echo $Var;  // Will output: World
```

4. **PHP Statements**:

o PHP statements end with a semicolon (;). This tells the interpreter that one statement has finished and the next one can begin.

36

Example:

```
php
```

```
echo "Hello, World!";  // Correct
echo  "Hello,  World!"      //  Incorrect:
Missing semicolon
```

Variables, Constants, and Data Types in PHP

In PHP, **variables** and **constants** are used to store data, and the language provides several data types to work with. Understanding these will allow you to manage data effectively in your PHP scripts.

1. **Variables**:
   o A variable in PHP starts with a dollar sign ($) followed by the variable name. PHP does not require you to define a type when declaring a variable, making it a **loosely typed** language.

   Example:

   ```
   php
   ```

   ```
   $message  =  "Hello,  World!";    //
   String variable
   ```

37

```
$age = 25;                          //
Integer variable
$isStudent = true;                  //
Boolean variable
```

- o **Variable Naming Rules**:
  - Variable names must start with a letter or an underscore (_).
  - They can contain letters, numbers, and underscores.
  - PHP variable names are case-sensitive.

2. **Constants**:
   - o A **constant** is similar to a variable, but its value cannot be changed once it's set. Constants are defined using the `define()` function.
   - o Constants do not require a dollar sign ($) in front of their name.

   Example:

   php

   ```
   define("SITE_NAME", "My Website");
   echo SITE_NAME;    // Outputs: My
   Website
   ```

3. **Data Types**: PHP supports several data types, including:

- o **String**: Text data, enclosed in single (') or double
  (") quotes.

```php
$name = "John Doe";
```

- o **Integer**: Whole numbers (positive or negative).

```php
$age = 30;
```

- o **Float (Double)**: Numbers with decimal points.

```php
$price = 19.99;
```

- o **Boolean**: Represents true or false values.

```php
$isActive = true;
```

- o **Array**: An ordered collection of values, which
  can be indexed or associative.

```php
```

```php
$fruits = array("Apple", "Banana",
"Orange");
```

- o **Object**: Instances of classes used in Object-Oriented Programming (OOP).
- o **NULL**: Represents a variable with no value.

```php
php

$var = NULL;
```

Introduction to Operators

Operators are used in PHP to perform operations on variables and values. They are essential for manipulating data, making comparisons, and controlling the flow of your application.

1. **Arithmetic Operators**:
   - o These operators perform basic mathematical operations.

```php
php

$a = 10;
$b = 5;
echo $a + $b;  // Addition: Outputs 15
```

```
echo $a - $b;      // Subtraction:
Outputs 5
echo $a * $b;      // Multiplication:
Outputs 50
echo $a / $b;  // Division: Outputs
2
echo $a % $b;          // Modulus
(remainder): Outputs 0
```

2. **Assignment Operators**:

   o   These operators assign values to variables.

   ```
   php
   ```

   ```
   $x = 10;        // Assign 10 to $x
   $x += 5;        // $x = $x + 5 (Result:
   15)
   $x -= 3;        // $x = $x - 3 (Result:
   12)
   ```

3. **Comparison Operators**:

   o   These operators are used to compare two values.

   ```
   php
   ```

   ```
   $a = 5;
   $b = 10;
   var_dump($a == $b);    // Equal to:
   Outputs false
   ```

```php
var_dump($a != $b);  // Not equal to:
Outputs true
var_dump($a < $b);    // Less than:
Outputs true
var_dump($a >= $b);  // Greater than
or equal to: Outputs false
```

4. **Logical Operators**:
   - These operators are used to combine multiple conditions.

   php

   ```php
   $x = true;
   $y = false;
   var_dump($x && $y);  // Logical AND:
   Outputs false
   var_dump($x || $y);   // Logical OR:
   Outputs true
   var_dump(!$x);        // Logical NOT:
   Outputs false
   ```

5. **String Operators**:
   - Used to concatenate strings.

   php

   ```php
   $firstName = "John";
   $lastName = "Doe";
   ```

```
$fullName  =  $firstName  .  "  "  .
$lastName;       //   Concatenation:
Outputs "John Doe"
```

6. **Increment/Decrement Operators**:

    o   These operators increase or decrease a variable by one.

```php
$x = 5;
$x++;  // Increment: $x becomes 6
$x--;  // Decrement: $x becomes 5
```

By the end of this chapter, you should have a clear understanding of:

- How to write and run basic PHP scripts.
- The PHP syntax, including tags, comments, and semicolons.
- The role of variables, constants, and data types in PHP.
- How to use operators to perform various tasks in PHP.

This foundation will allow you to build more complex PHP scripts as you continue to explore the language.

CHAPTER 4

WORKING WITH FORMS AND USER INPUT

Creating Forms in HTML

Forms are essential for collecting user input on websites. HTML forms provide an interface for users to submit data to the server. PHP processes the data submitted via forms to make dynamic content, user interactions, and database management possible.

1. **Basic HTML Form**: An HTML form is created using the `<form>` tag. It can contain various form elements such as text fields, radio buttons, checkboxes, and submit buttons. Here's a basic example of a form:

    html

    ```
    <form action="process.php" method="POST">
        <label for="name">Name:</label>
        <input    type="text"    id="name"
    name="name"><br><br>

        <label for="email">Email:</label>
        <input    type="email"    id="email"
    name="email"><br><br>
    ```

44

```
<input type="submit" value="Submit">
</form>
```

- o The `<form>` tag defines the form itself.
- o The `action` attribute specifies the PHP file (in this case, `process.php`) that will process the data when the form is submitted.
- o The `method` attribute specifies how the form data will be sent. It can be either GET or POST.

2. **Form Elements**:

- o **Text Field**: `<input type="text">` for short user inputs (like a name).
- o **Email Field**: `<input type="email">` specifically for email addresses.
- o **Radio Button**: Allows users to choose one option from a set. Example:

```
html
```

```
<input type="radio" name="gender"
value="male"> Male
<input type="radio" name="gender"
value="female"> Female
```

- o **Checkbox**: Lets users select multiple options. Example:

```
html
```

45

```
<input                type="checkbox"
name="newsletter"        value="yes">
Subscribe to newsletter
```

Processing Form Data with PHP

Once a user submits a form, the data is sent to the server, where PHP processes it. Depending on the method specified in the form (GET or POST), PHP will access the submitted data through the global $_GET or $_POST arrays.

1. **Using PHP to Access Form Data**: If the form uses the POST method, you can access form data like this:

   php

   ```php
   $name = $_POST['name'];
   $email = $_POST['email'];
   echo "Hello, " . $name . "! Your email is
   " . $email;
   ```

2. **Form Handling Example**: Here's a simple PHP script (process.php) to process the form data:

   php

   ```php
   <?php
   ```

46

```php
if      ($_SERVER["REQUEST_METHOD"]      ==
"POST") {
        // Collect and sanitize data
        $name                            =
htmlspecialchars($_POST['name']);
        $email                           =
htmlspecialchars($_POST['email']);
        echo "Name: " . $name . "<br>";
        echo "Email: " . $email;
    }
?>
```

- o `$_POST['name']` retrieves the form data submitted via the `POST` method.
- o **`htmlspecialchars()`** is used to convert special characters into HTML entities, protecting against **XSS (Cross-Site Scripting)** attacks.

3. **GET vs. POST Methods**:
   - o **GET**: Data is sent as part of the URL, making it visible to the user. It is generally used for non-sensitive data (e.g., search queries). For example: `http://example.com/process.php?name=John&email=john@example.com`
   - o **POST**: Data is sent through HTTP headers, making it more secure than GET since the data is not visible in the URL. POST is typically used for sensitive data (e.g., passwords).

47

Sanitizing and Validating User Input

When accepting input from users, it's essential to sanitize and validate the data to ensure its integrity and security. Unsanitized data can lead to various security issues, such as SQL injection or Cross-Site Scripting (XSS).

1. **Sanitizing Input**: Sanitizing means cleaning the data to ensure it doesn't contain unwanted characters or malicious code.

   o **HTML Special Characters**: Use `htmlspecialchars()` to convert special characters into HTML entities.

   ```php
   $name = htmlspecialchars($_POST['name']);
   ```

   o **Remove Unwanted Characters**: Use `filter_var()` for specific sanitization, like removing illegal characters.

   ```php
   $email = filter_var($_POST['email'], FILTER_SANITIZE_EMAIL);
   ```

2. **Validating Input**: Validation ensures that the input conforms to the expected format. For example, if a user submits an email, you want to ensure it's a valid email address.

   o **Email Validation**:

   php

```php
if              (filter_var($email,
FILTER_VALIDATE_EMAIL)) {
    echo "Valid email address.";
} else {
    echo "Invalid email address.";
}
```

   o **Required Fields**: Check if the user has filled in all the necessary fields.

   php

```php
if (empty($_POST['name'])) {
    echo "Name is required.";
}
```

3. **Common Functions for Sanitizing and Validating**:

   o **filter_var()**: Used for sanitization and validation.

   php

49

```
$email = filter_var($_POST['email'],
FILTER_SANITIZE_EMAIL);
if              (!filter_var($email,
FILTER_VALIDATE_EMAIL)) {
    echo "Invalid email format.";
}
```

o **preg_match()**: Used for custom pattern matching, useful for validating complex formats.

```
php
```

```
if  (preg_match("/^[a-zA-Z   ]*$/",
$_POST['name'])) {
    echo "Name is valid.";
} else {
    echo "Only  letters  and  white
space are allowed.";
}
```

Handling GET and POST Methods

Understanding how to handle GET and POST methods is key when dealing with form submissions. Both methods allow data to be sent to the server, but they differ in how the data is transmitted.

1. **GET Method**:

- o The data is appended to the URL, making it visible to the user.
- o Typically used for non-sensitive information (like search queries or pagination).
- o **Example**:

html

```
<form                    method="GET"
action="process.php">
    <input               type="text"
name="search">
    <input               type="submit"
value="Search">
</form>
```

In `process.php`, you can access the data using `$_GET`:

php

```
$search = $_GET['search'];
echo "You searched for: " . $search;
```

2. **POST Method**:

- o Data is sent in the HTTP request body, so it's not visible in the URL.
- o Used for sensitive data such as passwords, personal details, or file uploads.

o **Example**:

```
html
```

```
<form                    method="POST"
action="process.php">
    <input type="text" name="name">
    <input               type="submit"
value="Submit">
</form>
```

In `process.php`, you can access the data using `$_POST`:

```
php
```

```
$name = $_POST['name'];
echo "Hello, " . $name;
```

3. **When to Use GET vs POST**:

   o **GET**: Best suited for retrieving data (like search queries or links to pages). It's suitable when the data is not sensitive.

   o **POST**: Use when submitting sensitive information or when the data involves changes to the server (like user registration, login, or form submissions).

By the end of this chapter, you should be able to:

- Create forms in HTML for collecting user input.
- Process form data in PHP using the GET and POST methods.
- Sanitize and validate user input to ensure security and data integrity.
- Understand when to use GET and POST based on the nature of the data.

These skills will form the foundation of many dynamic PHP applications, allowing you to interact with users and handle their data securely and effectively.

CHAPTER 5

PHP AND MYSQL: INTRODUCTION TO DATABASES

Overview of Databases and SQL

Databases are essential for storing, retrieving, and manipulating data in web applications. A **database** is essentially a structured collection of data that can be accessed, modified, and managed through a database management system (DBMS).

1. **What is a Database?**
   A **database** stores data in an organized way, typically using tables, rows, and columns. The data is structured to allow for efficient querying and management. For example, a database for an e-commerce website might have tables for products, customers, and orders.
   - **Tables**: Each table contains rows and columns. Rows represent records, while columns represent fields (such as names, prices, or dates).
   - **Keys**: A **primary key** is a unique identifier for each record in a table, while a **foreign key** connects related data between tables.

2. **What is SQL (Structured Query Language)?** SQL is the language used to interact with relational databases like

54

MySQL. It allows you to create, modify, and query data within databases. Here are the main types of SQL operations:

- o **Data Definition Language (DDL)**: Defines database structure (e.g., CREATE, ALTER, DROP).

- o **Data Manipulation Language (DML)**: Manipulates the data (e.g., INSERT, UPDATE, DELETE).

- o **Data Query Language (DQL)**: Queries the data (e.g., SELECT).

3. **Relational Databases**: Relational databases store data in tables and support the use of **SQL** to manage the data. The data in one table can be related to data in another table using **foreign keys**. **MySQL** is one of the most popular relational databases and is widely used in web development.

Example:

- o **Table: Users**

user_id	name	email
1	John	john@example.com
2	Sarah	sarah@example.com

Connecting PHP to MySQL

In PHP, you can connect to a MySQL database using either the **MySQLi** (MySQL Improved) extension or **PDO (PHP Data Objects)**. Both provide a way to communicate with the MySQL database and execute SQL queries.

1. **Using MySQLi**: The MySQLi extension provides a simple way to interact with MySQL databases. You can use **procedural** or **object-oriented** style with MySQLi.

   o **Procedural Approach**:

   php

   ```php
   <?php
   // Connect to MySQL database
   $conn = mysqli_connect("localhost", "username", "password", "database_name");

   // Check connection
   if (!$conn) {
       die("Connection failed: " . mysqli_connect_error());
   }
   echo "Connected successfully";
   ?>
   ```

   o **Object-Oriented Approach**:

```
php
```

```php
<?php
// Create a new MySQLi object
$conn = new mysqli("localhost",
"username", "password",
"database_name");

// Check connection
if ($conn->connect_error) {
    die("Connection failed: " .
$conn->connect_error);
}
echo "Connected successfully";
?>
```

- o **Connection Parameters**:
    - `localhost`: The server where the MySQL database is hosted.
    - `username`: The MySQL username.
    - `password`: The password for the MySQL user.
    - `database_name`: The name of the database to which you are connecting.

2. **Using PDO**: The **PDO** extension provides a consistent interface for accessing different types of databases, including MySQL. It is more flexible than MySQLi

because it allows you to connect to multiple database types.

php

```php
<?php
try {
    // Create a new PDO instance
    $conn                =                 new
PDO("mysql:host=localhost;dbname=database
_name", "username", "password");

    // Set the PDO error mode to exception
    $conn-
>setAttribute(PDO::ATTR_ERRMODE,
PDO::ERRMODE_EXCEPTION);
    echo "Connected successfully";
} catch (PDOException $e) {
    echo "Connection failed: "  . $e-
>getMessage();
}
?>
```

- o **Benefits of PDO**:
    - Works with multiple database systems (e.g., MySQL, PostgreSQL, SQLite).
    - Supports named placeholders and prepared statements for better security and efficiency.

58

Performing Basic CRUD Operations (Create, Read, Update, Delete)

CRUD operations are fundamental for interacting with a database. These operations allow you to create, read, update, and delete records in your MySQL database using PHP.

1. **Create (Insert Data)**: The **INSERT** statement is used to add new records to a database table. Here's how you can insert data into a `users` table using PHP.

   MySQL Query:

   ```sql
   INSERT INTO users (name, email) VALUES ('John', 'john@example.com');
   ```

   PHP Code:

   ```php
   <?php
   $conn = mysqli_connect("localhost", "username", "password", "database_name");

   if (!$conn) {
       die("Connection failed: " . mysqli_connect_error());
   ```

```php
}

$name = "John";
$email = "john@example.com";
$sql = "INSERT INTO users (name, email)
VALUES ('$name', '$email')";

if (mysqli_query($conn, $sql)) {
    echo "New record created
successfully";
} else {
    echo "Error: " . $sql . "<br>" .
mysqli_error($conn);
}

mysqli_close($conn);
?>
```

- o **Prepared Statements**: Using prepared statements helps prevent **SQL injection** attacks. It binds the data parameters separately from the SQL query.

  php

```php
$stmt = $conn->prepare("INSERT INTO
users (name, email) VALUES (?, ?)");
```

```
$stmt->bind_param("ss",        $name,
$email);  // "ss" denotes two string
parameters
$stmt->execute();
```

2. **Read (Retrieve Data)**: The **SELECT** statement retrieves data from the database. You can use PHP to fetch the data and display it on a web page.

MySQL Query:

```sql
sql

SELECT * FROM users;
```

PHP Code:

```php
php

<?php
$conn    =    mysqli_connect("localhost",
"username", "password", "database_name");

if (!$conn) {
    die("Connection    failed:    "    .
mysqli_connect_error());
}

$sql = "SELECT * FROM users";
$result = mysqli_query($conn, $sql);
```

```
if (mysqli_num_rows($result) > 0) {
    while($row                          =
mysqli_fetch_assoc($result)) {
        echo "id: " . $row["id"]. " - Name:
"  .  $row["name"].  "  -  Email:  "  .
$row["email"]. "<br>";
    }
} else {
    echo "0 results";
}

mysqli_close($conn);
?>
```

3. **Update (Modify Data)**: The **UPDATE** statement modifies existing records in the database.

MySQL Query:

```
sql
```

```
UPDATE            users            SET
email='newemail@example.com' WHERE id=1;
```

PHP Code:

```
php
```

```
<?php
```

```
$conn     =     mysqli_connect("localhost",
"username", "password", "database_name");

if (!$conn) {
    die("Connection     failed:     "    .
mysqli_connect_error());
}

$newEmail = "newemail@example.com";
$id = 1;
$sql = "UPDATE users SET email='$newEmail'
WHERE id=$id";

if (mysqli_query($conn, $sql)) {
    echo "Record updated successfully";
} else {
    echo  "Error  updating  record:  "  .
mysqli_error($conn);
}

mysqli_close($conn);
?>
```

4. **Delete (Remove Data)**: The **DELETE** statement removes records from the database.

MySQL Query:

```
sql
```

63

```
DELETE FROM users WHERE id=1;
```

PHP Code:

```
php

<?php
$conn    =    mysqli_connect("localhost",
"username", "password", "database_name");

if (!$conn) {
    die("Connection    failed:    "    .
mysqli_connect_error());
}

$id = 1;
$sql = "DELETE FROM users WHERE id=$id";

if (mysqli_query($conn, $sql)) {
    echo "Record deleted successfully";
} else {
    echo  "Error  deleting  record:  "  .
mysqli_error($conn);
}

mysqli_close($conn);
?>
```

By the end of this chapter, you should be able to:

- Understand the basics of databases and SQL.
- Connect PHP to a MySQL database.
- Perform basic CRUD operations (Create, Read, Update, Delete) in PHP using MySQL.

These foundational skills will help you manage data within your PHP applications, providing you with the tools to build dynamic, database-driven websites and applications.

CHAPTER 6

ARRAYS AND LOOPS IN PHP

Working with Indexed and Associative Arrays

In PHP, **arrays** are used to store multiple values in a single variable. Arrays are one of the most powerful data structures in PHP, allowing you to group related data together for easy management. There are two main types of arrays in PHP: **indexed arrays** and **associative arrays**.

1. **Indexed Arrays**: Indexed arrays are arrays where the elements are stored with numeric indexes. These indexes are automatically assigned by PHP, starting from 0 by default.

   Example of an Indexed Array:

   php

   ```php
   <?php
   $fruits   =   array("Apple",   "Banana",
   "Orange");
   echo $fruits[0];  // Outputs: Apple
   echo $fruits[1];  // Outputs: Banana
   echo $fruits[2];  // Outputs: Orange
   ?>
   ```

66

In this example, the array $fruits holds three string values, and PHP automatically assigns the index starting from 0 (i.e., "Apple" is at index 0, "Banana" is at index 1, and so on).

2. **Associative Arrays**: Associative arrays are arrays where each element is associated with a unique **key** instead of a numeric index. The keys are usually strings, but they can be numbers as well.

    Example of an Associative Array:

    php

    ```php
    <?php
    $person = array(
        "name" => "John",
        "age" => 25,
        "email" => "john@example.com"
    );
    echo $person["name"];   // Outputs: John
    echo $person["age"];    // Outputs: 25
    echo    $person["email"];    //    Outputs:
    john@example.com
    ?>
    ```

    In this example, the array $person contains key-value pairs where "name", "age", and "email" are the keys, and the associated values are "John", 25, and "john@example.com", respectively.

Iterating Through Arrays Using Loops (for, foreach, while)

PHP provides several ways to iterate over arrays, allowing you to loop through all the elements and perform actions on them.

1. **Using `for` Loop**: The `for` loop is used when you know the exact number of iterations, typically when dealing with indexed arrays.

   Example:

   php

   ```php
   <?php
   $fruits     =    array("Apple",    "Banana",
   "Orange");

   for ($i = 0; $i < count($fruits); $i++) {
       echo $fruits[$i] . "<br>";
   }
   ?>
   ```

   o The `for` loop starts with `$i = 0` and continues until `$i` is less than the length of the array (count($fruits)), outputting each element one by one.

2. **Using `foreach` Loop**: The foreach loop is specifically designed for arrays and is the easiest way to iterate through all elements in an array.

Example (Indexed Array):

php

```php
<?php
$fruits    =    array("Apple",    "Banana",
"Orange");

foreach ($fruits as $fruit) {
    echo $fruit . "<br>";
}
?>
```

  o In this example, $fruit will hold each value of the array in turn (i.e., "Apple", then "Banana", then "Orange").

Example (Associative Array):

php

```php
<?php
$person = array(
```

69

```php
    "name" => "John",
    "age" => 25,
    "email" => "john@example.com"
);


foreach ($person as $key => $value) {
    echo "$key: $value<br>";
}
?>
```

- o Here, `$key` holds the array key (e.g., `"name"`), and `$value` holds the associated value (e.g., `"John"`).

3. **Using `while` Loop**: The `while` loop is another option for iterating through arrays. It is typically used when you don't know the exact number of iterations beforehand and will continue looping until a condition is met.

Example:

php

```php
<?php
$fruits  =   array("Apple",   "Banana",
"Orange");
$i = 0;

while ($i < count($fruits)) {
    echo $fruits[$i] . "<br>";
```

70

```
        $i++;
    }
    ?>
```

Multidimensional Arrays

A **multidimensional array** is an array that contains one or more arrays as elements. It is useful for storing complex data, like tables, matrices, or records with multiple properties.

1. **Creating a Multidimensional Array**: You can create multidimensional arrays using a combination of indexed and associative arrays. For example, a **2D array** can represent a table with rows and columns.

   Example:

```php
<?php
$contacts = array(
    array("John",     "john@example.com",
"555-1234"),
    array("Sarah",    "sarah@example.com",
"555-5678"),
    array("Mike",     "mike@example.com",
"555-8765")
);
```

71

```
echo $contacts[0][0];  // Outputs: John
echo    $contacts[1][1];       //    Outputs:
sarah@example.com
?>
```

- o $contacts[0][0] accesses the first element in the first row ("John").
- o $contacts[1][1] accesses the second element in the second row ("sarah@example.com").

2. **Iterating Through Multidimensional Arrays**: To loop through a multidimensional array, you can use nested loops.

   Example:

   php

```
<?php
$contacts = array(
    array("John",      "john@example.com",
"555-1234"),
    array("Sarah",     "sarah@example.com",
"555-5678"),
    array("Mike",      "mike@example.com",
"555-8765")
);

foreach ($contacts as $contact) {
```

```
echo "Name: " . $contact[0] . "<br>";
echo "Email: " . $contact[1] . "<br>";
echo "Phone: " . $contact[2] .
"<br><br>";
}
?>
```

Sorting and Manipulating Arrays

PHP provides several built-in functions to manipulate and sort arrays, making it easier to handle large datasets.

1. **Sorting Arrays**: PHP offers several functions to sort arrays, such as:

    o **sort()**: Sorts an indexed array in ascending order.

        php

        ```php
        <?php
        $fruits = array("Banana", "Apple",
        "Orange");
        sort($fruits);
        print_r($fruits);  // Outputs: Array
        ( [0] => Apple [1] => Banana [2] =>
        Orange )
        ?>
        ```

73

- **asort()**: Sorts an associative array by value, maintaining the key-value associations.

php

```php
<?php
$person = array("age" => 25, "name"
=>      "John",      "email"      =>
"john@example.com");
asort($person);
print_r($person);  // Outputs: Array
( [name] => John [age] => 25 [email]
=> john@example.com )
?>
```

- **ksort()**: Sorts an associative array by key.

php

```php
<?php
$person = array("age" => 25, "name"
=>      "John",      "email"      =>
"john@example.com");
ksort($person);
print_r($person);  // Outputs: Array
(   [age]   =>   25   [email]   =>
john@example.com [name] => John )
?>
```

2. **Reversing an Array**: You can reverse an array using the `array_reverse()` function.

php

```php
<?php
$fruits   =   array("Apple",   "Banana",
"Orange");
$reversedFruits = array_reverse($fruits);
print_r($reversedFruits);    // Outputs:
Array ( [0] => Orange [1] => Banana [2] =>
Apple )
?>
```

3. **Array Manipulation Functions**:
   - o **array_merge()**: Merges two or more arrays into one.

     php

     ```php
     <?php
     $array1 = array("a" => "apple", "b"
     => "banana");
     $array2 = array("c" => "cherry", "d"
     => "date");
     $merged   =   array_merge($array1,
     $array2);
     ```

```
print_r($merged);  // Outputs: Array
( [a] => apple [b] => banana [c] =>
cherry [d] => date )
?>
```

○ **array_slice()**: Extracts a portion of an array.

php

```
<?php
$fruits = array("Apple", "Banana",
"Orange", "Grape");
$sliced = array_slice($fruits, 1,
2);
print_r($sliced);  // Outputs: Array
( [0] => Banana [1] => Orange )
?>
```

By the end of this chapter, you should be able to:

- Understand the difference between indexed and associative arrays in PHP.
- Loop through arrays using for, foreach, and while loops.
- Work with multidimensional arrays to store complex data.
- Sort, manipulate, and reverse arrays using built-in PHP functions.

These skills are foundational for handling data in PHP, and mastering arrays will help you efficiently manage and display large datasets in your applications.

CHAPTER 7

FUNCTIONS IN PHP

Creating and Using Functions

Functions are one of the most powerful features in PHP, enabling you to group related tasks into reusable blocks of code. A function in PHP is defined using the `function` keyword, followed by the function name and a pair of parentheses `()`.

1. **Defining a Function**: A function in PHP consists of a declaration and a body. The declaration specifies the function's name, and the body contains the code that the function will execute.

   Example:

   php

   ```php
   <?php
   function greet() {
       echo "Hello, World!";
   }

   // Calling the function
   greet();  // Outputs: Hello, World!
   ?>
   ```

In this example:

- o   `function greet()` defines a function named `greet`.
- o   The function contains the code `echo "Hello, World!"`, which prints a message to the screen.
- o   The function is called using `greet();`, which executes the code inside the function body.

2. **Function with Parameters**: Functions can accept input values, known as **parameters**, to make them more flexible. Parameters are specified inside the parentheses when the function is declared.

Example:

php

```php
<?php
function greet($name) {
    echo "Hello, $name!";
}


greet("John");  // Outputs: Hello, John!
greet("Sarah"); // Outputs: Hello, Sarah!
?>
```

In this example:

79

- o The `greet()` function accepts a parameter `$name`.

- o When calling `greet()`, a string (`"John"`, `"Sarah"`) is passed to the `$name` parameter, which is then displayed in the message.

Understanding Function Parameters and Return Values

1. **Function Parameters**: Parameters are variables defined in the function declaration that allow you to pass data into the function. They make your function more flexible and reusable.

   - o **Type of Parameters**:
     - ▪ **Required Parameters**: These are parameters that must be passed when calling the function.
     - ▪ **Optional Parameters (Default Values)**: You can assign default values to parameters, which makes them optional when calling the function.

   Example with Optional Parameters:

   php

   ```
   <?php
   function greet($name = "Guest") {
   ```

```
        echo "Hello, $name!";
}

greet();              // Outputs: Hello,
Guest!
greet("John");  //  Outputs:  Hello,
John!
?>
```

2. **Return Values**: A function can return a value back to the caller using the `return` keyword. The return value can be of any data type (string, integer, array, etc.).

Example:

php

```
<?php
function add($a, $b) {
    return $a + $b;
}

$sum = add(5, 3);  // Calling the function
echo $sum;         // Outputs: 8
?>
```

In this example:

- o The add() function takes two parameters ($a and $b), adds them together, and returns the result.
- o The return value is assigned to the variable $sum, which is then printed to the screen.

3. **Returning Multiple Values**: If you need to return multiple values from a function, you can use an **array** or **associative array** to return several values at once.

Example:

php

```php
<?php
function getCoordinates() {
    return array(10, 20);   // Returning
multiple values as an array
}

list($x, $y) = getCoordinates();   //
Unpacking the array into variables
echo "X: $x, Y: $y";  // Outputs: X: 10, Y:
20
?>
```

82

Variable Scope and Global Variables

1. **Variable Scope**: PHP has different **scopes** for variables, determining where a variable can be accessed within the program.

   o **Local Scope**: Variables declared inside a function are local to that function and cannot be accessed outside of it.

   php

   ```php
   <?php
   function myFunction() {
       $localVar = "I am local!";
       echo $localVar;  // Outputs: I am local!
   }

   myFunction();
   echo $localVar;  // Error: Undefined variable
   ?>
   ```

   o **Global Scope**: Variables declared outside of functions are **global** and can be accessed anywhere in the script, but not directly inside functions.

   Example:

83

```
php

<?php
$globalVar = "I am global!";

function myFunction() {
    global $globalVar;
    echo $globalVar;   // Outputs: I
am global!
}

myFunction();
echo $globalVar;   // Outputs: I am
global!
?>
```

- **global Keyword**: To access a global variable inside a function, you must use the global keyword. Alternatively, you can use the $GLOBALS superglobal array to access global variables.

Using $GLOBALS:

```
php

<?php
$globalVar = "I am global!";
function myFunction() {
```

```
        echo $GLOBALS['globalVar'];   //
Outputs: I am global!
}


myFunction();
?>
```

2. **Static Variables**:

   o A **static variable** retains its value between function calls. Normally, local variables are destroyed once the function ends, but static variables preserve their values.

   Example:

```
php

<?php
function counter() {
    static $count = 0;
    $count++;
    echo $count . "<br>";
}

counter();   // Outputs: 1
counter();   // Outputs: 2
counter();   // Outputs: 3
?>
```

PHP Built-in Functions

PHP has a rich library of built-in functions that simplify many common programming tasks. These functions cover a wide range of areas, such as string manipulation, array handling, date and time functions, file handling, and more.

1. **String Functions**:
   - **`strlen()`**: Returns the length of a string.

     php

     ```php
     echo strlen("Hello, World!");   // Outputs: 13
     ```

   - **`strpos()`**: Finds the position of the first occurrence of a substring.

     php

     ```php
     echo strpos("Hello, World!", "World");  // Outputs: 7
     ```

   - **`str_replace()`**: Replaces occurrences of a string with another.

     php

```
echo    str_replace("World",    "PHP",
"Hello, World!");  // Outputs: Hello,
PHP!
```

2. **Array Functions**:

   o **count()**: Returns the number of elements in an array.

   php

   ```
   $fruits  =  array("Apple",  "Banana",
   "Orange");
   echo count($fruits);  // Outputs: 3
   ```

   o **array_merge()**: Merges two or more arrays.

   php

   ```
   $arr1 = array("a" => "apple", "b" =>
   "banana");
   $arr2 = array("c" => "cherry", "d" =>
   "date");
   $merged = array_merge($arr1, $arr2);
   print_r($merged);  // Outputs: Array
   ( [a] => apple [b] => banana [c] =>
   cherry [d] => date )
   ```

3. **Date and Time Functions**:

   o **date()**: Formats a local date and time.

php

```
echo date("Y-m-d H:i:s"); // Outputs
current date and time, e.g., 2023-
04-15 12:00:00
```

- **strtotime()**: Parses an English textual datetime description into a Unix timestamp.

php

```
echo strtotime("next Monday"); //
Outputs a timestamp for the next
Monday
```

4. **Mathematical Functions**:
   - **abs()**: Returns the absolute value of a number.

php

```
echo abs(-10); // Outputs: 10
```

   - **rand()**: Generates a random integer.

php

```
echo rand(1, 100); // Outputs a
random number between 1 and 100
```

5. **File Handling Functions**:

- o **fopen()**: Opens a file or URL.

```php
$file = fopen("example.txt", "r");
```

- o **file_get_contents()**: Reads a file into a string.

```php
echo
file_get_contents("example.txt");
```

By the end of this chapter, you should be able to:

- Create and use functions in PHP to organize and reuse code.
- Understand how function parameters and return values work.
- Work with variable scope and use global variables when necessary.
- Use some of PHP's built-in functions to simplify common tasks.

Mastering PHP functions will significantly enhance your ability to write clean, efficient, and maintainable code, making your web applications more modular and easier to manage.

CHAPTER 8

OBJECT-ORIENTED PROGRAMMING (OOP) IN PHP

Introduction to OOP Concepts (Classes, Objects, Inheritance)

Object-Oriented Programming (OOP) is a programming paradigm that organizes code into **objects** rather than functions and logic. These objects represent real-world entities and can contain both data and methods to manipulate that data. PHP supports OOP, allowing you to design web applications in a more modular and structured way.

1. **Classes and Objects**:
   - **Class**: A class is a blueprint for creating objects. It defines the properties (variables) and methods (functions) that an object will have.
   - **Object**: An object is an instance of a class. When you create an object, it is based on the structure defined in the class.

Example:

```php
php

<?php
```

90

```php
class Car {
    // Properties
    public $brand;
    public $color;

    // Constructor
    public function __construct($brand,
$color) {
        $this->brand = $brand;
        $this->color = $color;
    }

    // Method
    public function getDetails() {
        return "This is a " . $this->color
. " " . $this->brand;
    }
}

// Creating an object of the class
$car1 = new Car("Toyota", "Red");
echo $car1->getDetails();  // Outputs: This
is a Red Toyota
?>
```

- o **Explanation**:
  - class Car defines a class with two properties: $brand and $color.

91

- The `__construct` method initializes the object's properties.
- `getDetails()` is a method that returns the car's details.
- `new Car("Toyota", "Red")` creates an object `$car1` based on the `Car` class.

2. **Inheritance**:

   o Inheritance allows one class to inherit the properties and methods of another class. This helps in creating a hierarchy of classes and reusing code.

Example:

php

```php
<?php
class Vehicle {
    public $brand;
    public $color;

    public function __construct($brand, $color) {
        $this->brand = $brand;
        $this->color = $color;
    }

    public function getDetails() {
```

92

```php
        return "This is a " . $this->color
. " " . $this->brand;
    }
}


class Car extends Vehicle {
    public $model;

    public function __construct($brand,
$color, $model) {
        parent::__construct($brand,
$color);  // Inherit from Vehicle class
        $this->model = $model;
    }

    public function getCarDetails() {
        return $this->getDetails() . ",
model: " . $this->model;
    }
}


// Creating an object of the Car class
$car1 = new Car("Toyota", "Red",
"Corolla");
echo $car1->getCarDetails();  // Outputs:
This is a Red Toyota, model: Corolla
?>
```

   o **Explanation**:

93

- The Car class inherits from the Vehicle class using the extends keyword.
- The Car constructor calls the parent constructor to initialize the inherited properties ($brand, $color).
- getCarDetails() is a method specific to the Car class, and it uses the inherited getDetails() method.

Understanding Constructors and Destructors

1. **Constructors**:
   o A **constructor** is a special method that is automatically called when an object is created. It is typically used to initialize the properties of the object.

Example:

php

```php
<?php
class Book {
    public $title;
    public $author;

    // Constructor
```

94

```
    public   function   __construct($title,
$author) {
        $this->title = $title;
        $this->author = $author;
    }

    public function getBookDetails() {
        return "Title: " . $this->title .
", Author: " . $this->author;
    }
}

// Creating an object of the Book class
$book1 = new Book("The Great Gatsby", "F.
Scott Fitzgerald");
echo    $book1->getBookDetails();        //
Outputs: Title: The Great Gatsby, Author:
F. Scott Fitzgerald
?>
```

- o **Explanation**:
  - The __construct() method initializes the object properties $title and $author when a Book object is created.

2. **Destructors**:
   - o A **destructor** is another special method that is called when an object is destroyed or goes out of scope. It is typically used to perform cleanup

operations, such as closing database connections or releasing resources.

Example:

php

```php
<?php
class Book {
    public $title;
    public $author;

    // Constructor
    public function __construct($title,
$author) {
        $this->title = $title;
        $this->author = $author;
    }

    // Destructor
    public function __destruct() {
        echo "The book '$this->title' is
being destroyed.<br>";
    }

    public function getBookDetails() {
        return "Title: " . $this->title .
", Author: " . $this->author;
    }
```

```
}

// Creating an object of the Book class
$book1 = new Book("The Great Gatsby", "F.
Scott Fitzgerald");
echo    $book1->getBookDetails();        //
Outputs: Title: The Great Gatsby, Author:
F. Scott Fitzgerald

// The destructor is automatically called
when the object goes out of scope
?>
```

- o **Explanation**:
  - The __destruct() method is automatically called when the object $book1 is destroyed. In this case, it outputs a message when the object is cleaned up.

Working with Methods and Properties

1. **Methods**:
   - o A **method** is a function that is defined inside a class and is used to perform operations on the properties of the object or perform other actions.

Example:

php

```php
<?php
class Car {
    public $brand;
    public $color;

    // Constructor
    public function __construct($brand,
$color) {
        $this->brand = $brand;
        $this->color = $color;
    }

    // Method to display car details
    public function displayDetails() {
        return "This is a " . $this->color
. " " . $this->brand;
    }
}

$car = new Car("Toyota", "Red");
echo $car->displayDetails();   // Outputs:
This is a Red Toyota
?>
```

2. **Properties**:

o **Properties** are variables that are defined within a class. They hold the data or attributes for each object created from the class.

Example:

php

```php
<?php
class Person {
    public $name;
    public $age;

    // Constructor
    public function __construct($name, $age) {
        $this->name = $name;
        $this->age = $age;
    }
}

$person1 = new Person("John", 25);
echo $person1->name;  // Outputs: John
echo $person1->age;   // Outputs: 25
?>
```

99

Access Modifiers (Public, Private, Protected)

PHP provides **access modifiers** to control the visibility and accessibility of class properties and methods. These modifiers help encapsulate data and protect it from unauthorized access.

1. **Public**:
   - **Public** properties and methods are accessible from anywhere, both inside and outside the class.

   Example:

   php

   ```php
   <?php
   class Car {
       public $brand;

       public function __construct($brand) {
           $this->brand = $brand;
       }
   }

   $car = new Car("Toyota");
   echo $car->brand;   // Outputs: Toyota
   ?>
   ```

2. **Private**:

o **Private** properties and methods can only be accessed within the same class. They are not accessible outside the class, even by objects of the same class.

Example:

php

```php
<?php
class Car {
    private $brand;

    public function __construct($brand) {
        $this->brand = $brand;
    }

    public function getBrand() {
        return $this->brand;  // Accessing
private property within the class
    }
}

$car = new Car("Toyota");
echo $car->getBrand();  // Outputs: Toyota
// echo $car->brand;  // Error: Cannot
access private property
?>
```

3. **Protected**:

   o **Protected** properties and methods can be accessed within the same class and by subclasses (child classes). They are not accessible from outside the class unless through inheritance.

Example:

php

```php
<?php
class Vehicle {
    protected $brand;

    public function __construct($brand) {
        $this->brand = $brand;
    }
}

class Car extends Vehicle {
    public function getBrand() {
        return $this->brand;  // Accessing
protected property in the child class
    }
}

$car = new Car("Toyota");
echo $car->getBrand();  // Outputs: Toyota
?>
```

By the end of this chapter, you should be able to:

- Understand the basic principles of Object-Oriented Programming in PHP.
- Create and work with classes and objects.
- Use constructors and destructors to manage object initialization and cleanup.
- Work with methods and properties to define behavior and data for your objects.
- Understand and use access modifiers (public, private, protected) to control the visibility and access to properties and methods.

Mastering OOP in PHP is a powerful way to build scalable, maintainable, and reusable web applications.

CHAPTER 9

ADVANCED OBJECT-ORIENTED PHP

Static Methods and Properties

In Object-Oriented Programming (OOP), **static** methods and properties are tied to the class itself rather than instances (objects) of that class. This means you can access them without creating an object.

1. **Static Properties**: A static property belongs to the class rather than an instance of the class. It is shared by all instances of the class.

   Example:

   php

   ```php
   <?php
   class Car {
       public static $brand = "Toyota";

       public static function getBrand() {
           return self::$brand;
       }
   }
   ```

```
// Accessing   static   property   without
creating an instance
echo Car::$brand;  // Outputs: Toyota

// Accessing static method
echo Car::getBrand();  // Outputs: Toyota
?>
```

- o Car::$brand is a static property that can be accessed directly from the class without an object instance.
- o The getBrand() method is static and can also be called without creating an object.

2. **Static Methods**: A static method can only access other static properties or methods. It is called using the class name, and it doesn't need an instance to be invoked.

Example:

php

```
<?php
class Calculator {
    public static function add($a, $b) {
        return $a + $b;
    }
}
```

```
echo Calculator::add(5, 3);   // Outputs: 8
?>
```

- o Static methods are useful for utility functions, like performing calculations or logging, that don't need object-specific data.

Interfaces and Abstract Classes

Both **interfaces** and **abstract classes** are used to define blueprints for classes, but they serve different purposes and have different restrictions.

1. **Interfaces**: An **interface** defines a contract that a class must adhere to, meaning the class must implement all the methods declared in the interface. However, interfaces cannot contain properties or method implementations.

   Example:

   php

```
<?php
interface Vehicle {
    public function startEngine();
    public function stopEngine();
}
```

106

```
class Car implements Vehicle {
    public function startEngine() {
        echo "Car engine started<br>";
    }

    public function stopEngine() {
        echo "Car engine stopped<br>";
    }
}

$car = new Car();
$car->startEngine();    // Outputs: Car
engine started
$car->stopEngine();     // Outputs: Car
engine stopped
?>
```

- o **Key Points**:
  - ▪ A class that implements an interface must implement all the methods defined in the interface.
  - ▪ Interfaces cannot have method bodies; they only define the method signatures.

2. **Abstract Classes**: An **abstract class** is a class that cannot be instantiated directly. It can contain both abstract methods (which must be implemented by child classes) and concrete methods (methods with implementation). Abstract classes are used as a base class for other classes.

Example:

php

```php
<?php
abstract class Animal {
    public $name;

    abstract public function makeSound();

    public function setName($name) {
        $this->name = $name;
    }
}

class Dog extends Animal {
    public function makeSound() {
        echo "Woof!<br>";
    }
}

$dog = new Dog();
$dog->setName("Buddy");
echo $dog->name . "<br>";    // Outputs:
Buddy
$dog->makeSound();        // Outputs: Woof!
?>
```

o **Key Points**:

- An abstract class cannot be instantiated directly. You must create a subclass that implements the abstract methods.

- An abstract method is a method declared in an abstract class that does not have a body and must be implemented by the subclass.

Namespaces in PHP

Namespaces help avoid name conflicts by grouping logically related classes, functions, and constants under a unique name. They are particularly useful when working with large applications or external libraries.

1. **Defining and Using Namespaces**: You can define a namespace by using the `namespace` keyword at the beginning of a PHP file. To access elements from a namespace, you use the `use` keyword.

   Example:

   php

```php
<?php
namespace CarNamespace;
```

```php
class Car {
    public function drive() {
        echo "The car is driving.<br>";
    }
}

// Accessing the class from the namespace
$car = new Car();
$car->drive();    // Outputs: The car is
driving.
?>
```

o **Using Multiple Namespaces**:

php

```php
<?php
namespace VehicleNamespace;

class Vehicle {
    public function move() {
        echo    "The    vehicle    is
moving.<br>";
    }
}

namespace CarNamespace;

class Car {
    public function drive() {
```

110

```
        echo    "The     car     is
driving.<br>";
    }
}


// Accessing the classes from
different namespaces
$vehicle           =           new
\VehicleNamespace\Vehicle();
$vehicle->move();  // Outputs: The
vehicle is moving.

$car = new \CarNamespace\Car();
$car->drive();  // Outputs: The car
is driving.
?>
```

2. **Aliases with use**: You can also create aliases for namespaces to make them easier to use.

Example:

```
php

<?php
namespace AnimalNamespace;

class Dog {
    public function speak() {
        echo "Woof!<br>";
```

111

```
        }

    }


    // Alias the class to a shorter name
    use AnimalNamespace\Dog as Puppy;

    $dog = new Puppy();
    $dog->speak();   // Outputs: Woof!
    ?>
```

- o **Key Points**:
    - Namespaces prevent name conflicts between classes, functions, or constants with the same name in different parts of your application.
    - The use keyword allows you to import classes or functions from namespaces into your current script.

Exception Handling in PHP

Exception handling in PHP is used to manage errors and exceptional conditions in a structured way. Instead of PHP's default error handling, exceptions allow for cleaner, more understandable error management.

1. **Throwing Exceptions**: The `throw` keyword is used to create an exception. An exception is an object that is thrown when an error occurs.

   Example:

   php

   ```php
   <?php
   function checkAge($age) {
       if ($age < 18) {
           throw new Exception("You must be 18 or older.");
       }
       return "You are old enough.";
   }

   try {
       echo checkAge(16);
   } catch (Exception $e) {
       echo 'Caught exception: ', $e->getMessage();   // Outputs: Caught exception: You must be 18 or older.
   }
   ?>
   ```

   - **Key Points**:
     - An exception is thrown when a certain condition is met (e.g., age is less than 18).

113

- The `try` block contains code that may throw an exception, and the `catch` block handles the exception.

2. **Catching Exceptions**: You can catch exceptions using a `try-catch` block. When an exception is thrown, the flow of the program moves to the `catch` block, where you can handle the error gracefully.

Example:

php

```php
<?php
try {
    // Some code that may throw an exception
    throw new Exception("Something went wrong!");
} catch (Exception $e) {
    echo "Caught exception: " . $e->getMessage();  // Outputs: Caught exception: Something went wrong!
}
?>
```

3. **Custom Exception Classes**: You can create your own custom exception class by extending the built-in `Exception` class.

114

Example:

php

```php
<?php
class CustomException extends Exception {
    public function errorMessage() {
        return "Custom Error: " . $this-
>getMessage();
    }
}

try {
    throw new CustomException("This is a
custom exception.");
} catch (CustomException $e) {
    echo $e->errorMessage();   // Outputs:
Custom Error: This is a custom exception.
}
?>
```

4. **Finally Block**: The `finally` block is optional and is executed after the `try` and `catch` blocks, regardless of whether an exception was thrown or not. It is typically used for cleanup operations.

Example:

php

```php
<?php
try {
    echo "Trying something<br>";
    // throw new Exception("An error
occurred.");
} catch (Exception $e) {
    echo "Caught exception: ", $e-
>getMessage();
} finally {
    echo "<br>Finally block executed.";
}
?>
```

By the end of this chapter, you should be able to:

- Work with **static methods and properties** for data and methods tied to the class rather than instances.
- Understand **interfaces** and **abstract classes** to define contracts and reusable base classes.
- Use **namespaces** to prevent name conflicts in your code and create modular code.
- Implement **exception handling** to manage errors and ensure your PHP applications can handle unexpected situations gracefully.

Mastering these advanced OOP concepts will help you build scalable, maintainable, and robust PHP applications.

116

CHAPTER 10

WORKING WITH FILES IN PHP

Reading from and Writing to Files

PHP provides a variety of functions for working with files. This includes reading from files, writing to files, and appending data to existing files. PHP allows you to perform file operations in both **text mode** and **binary mode**.

1. **Opening a File**:
   o You use the `fopen()` function to open a file in PHP. The `fopen()` function takes two arguments:
      ▪ The file name or path.
      ▪ The mode in which to open the file (e.g., read, write, append).

   Example:

   php

   ```php
   <?php
   $file = fopen("example.txt", "r");   // Opens the file in read mode
   if (!$file) {
       echo "Failed to open the file.";
   ```

117

```
} else {
    echo "File opened successfully!";
}
fclose($file);  // Close the file
?>
```

2. **Reading from a File**: PHP provides several functions to read the contents of a file.

   o **fgets()**: Reads a single line from a file.

   php

   ```
   <?php
   $file = fopen("example.txt", "r");
   while ($line = fgets($file)) {
       echo $line . "<br>";
   }
   fclose($file);
   ?>
   ```

   o **fread()**: Reads a specific number of bytes from a file.

   php

   ```
   <?php
   $file = fopen("example.txt", "r");
   $content     =        fread($file,
   filesize("example.txt"));   // Read
   the entire file
   ```

```
echo $content;
fclose($file);
?>
```

- o **file_get_contents()**: A simpler way to read the entire file into a string.

```
php
```

```php
<?php
$content                          =
file_get_contents("example.txt");
echo $content;
?>
```

3. **Writing to a File**:

- o **fwrite()**: Writes data to a file. If the file doesn't exist, PHP can create it.

```
php
```

```php
<?php
$file = fopen("example.txt", "w");
// Open file in write mode (creates
the file if it doesn't exist)
if ($file) {
    fwrite($file, "Hello, world!");
    fclose($file);  // Always close
the file after writing
}
```

```
?>
```

o **file_put_contents()**: A simpler function to write data to a file.

php

```
<?php
file_put_contents("example.txt",
"This is the new content.");
?>
```

o **Appending to a File**: To append data to an existing file (instead of overwriting it), use the mode "a" (append mode) with fopen() or the file_put_contents() function with the FILE_APPEND flag.

php

```
<?php
$file = fopen("example.txt", "a");
// Open file in append mode
fwrite($file, "\nAppending this
text.");
fclose($file);
?>
```

Handling File Uploads and Downloads

File uploads and downloads are crucial for web applications, such as when users upload images, documents, or download files from your server.

1. **File Uploads**: In PHP, you can handle file uploads via the `$_FILES` superglobal array. This array contains information about the uploaded file, such as its name, type, size, and temporary location on the server.

   o **HTML Form for File Upload**:

   ```html
   html
   ```

   ```html
   <form            action="upload.php"
   method="POST"
   enctype="multipart/form-data">
       <input              type="file"
   name="fileToUpload"
   id="fileToUpload">
       <input            type="submit"
   value="Upload File" name="submit">
   </form>
   ```

   o **PHP Script to Handle the Upload** (`upload.php`):

   ```php
   php
   ```

121

```php
<?php
if ($_SERVER["REQUEST_METHOD"] ==
"POST") {
    $target_dir = "uploads/";
    $target_file = $target_dir .
basename($_FILES["fileToUpload"]["n
ame"]);

    // Check if the file is uploaded
    if
(move_uploaded_file($_FILES["fileTo
Upload"]["tmp_name"], $target_file))
{
        echo "The file " .
basename($_FILES["fileToUpload"]["n
ame"]) . " has been uploaded.";
    } else {
        echo "Sorry, there was an
error uploading your file.";
    }
}
?>
```

- **Explanation**:
  - $_FILES["fileToUpload"]
    ["tmp_name"]: This contains
    the temporary location of the
    uploaded file.

122

- move_uploaded_file():
  This function moves the uploaded file from the temporary location to the desired location (in this case, the uploads/ directory).

2. **File Downloads**: To allow users to download files from the server, PHP can serve the file by setting appropriate headers and reading the file content.

   o **Download Script**:

```
php
```

```php
<?php
$file = "uploads/example.txt";   //
File to download
if (file_exists($file)) {
    header('Content-Description:
File Transfer');
    header('Content-Type:
application/octet-stream');
    header('Content-Disposition:
attachment;        filename="'     .
basename($file) . '"');
    header('Content-Length:    '    .
filesize($file));
    readfile($file);   // Output the
file content
```

123

```
    exit;
} else {
    echo "File not found.";
}
?>
```

- **Explanation**:
  - `Content-Type:`
    `application/octet-`
    `stream` specifies that the
    content is a file to be
    downloaded.
  - `Content-Disposition:`
    `attachment` prompts the
    browser to download the file,
    rather than display it.
  - `readfile()` reads and outputs
    the file content to the browser.

Directory Operations (Create, Read, Delete Directories)

PHP provides several functions to interact with directories,
enabling you to create, read, and delete directories on the server.

1. **Creating a Directory**: To create a directory, you can use
   the `mkdir()` function. You can also set the permissions
   for the new directory.

Example:

```
php
```

```php
<?php
if (!file_exists("new_directory")) {
    mkdir("new_directory", 0777, true);
// Create directory with permissions
    echo         "Directory         created
successfully.";
} else {
    echo "Directory already exists.";
}
?>
```

- o **Explanation**:
  - The `mkdir()` function creates a directory if it does not already exist.
  - The `0777` value specifies the directory's permissions (read, write, execute for owner, group, and others).
  - The `true` parameter allows the creation of nested directories (e.g., `mkdir("dir/subdir", 0777, true)`).

2. **Reading a Directory**: The `opendir()` function opens a directory, and `readdir()` is used to read the files within

125

it. The `closedir()` function is used to close the directory handle.

Example:

php

```php
<?php
$dir = "uploads/";
if ($handle = opendir($dir)) {
    while (($file = readdir($handle)) !==
false) {
        echo "Filename: $file<br>";
    }
    closedir($handle);
}
?>
```

- o **Explanation**:
  - `opendir()` opens the directory for reading.
  - `readdir()` reads the next entry in the directory.
  - `closedir()` closes the directory handle once you're done reading.

3. **Deleting a Directory**: To delete a directory, you can use `rmdir()`, but the directory must be empty. If it contains

files, you must first delete the files before deleting the directory.

Example:

php

```php
<?php
$dir = "uploads/temp_dir";
if (is_dir($dir)) {
    rmdir($dir);  // Removes the directory
(must be empty)
    echo        "Directory        deleted
successfully.";
} else {
    echo "Directory does not exist.";
}
?>
```

- o **Explanation**:
  - ▪ rmdir() removes the specified empty directory.
  - ▪ The is_dir() function checks if the directory exists before attempting to delete it.

Summary

By the end of this chapter, you should be able to:

- Read from and write to files using functions like `fopen()`, `fgets()`, `fwrite()`, and `file_put_contents()`.
- Handle file uploads and downloads, including validating and moving files using `move_uploaded_file()` and setting appropriate headers for file downloads.
- Perform basic directory operations, including creating, reading, and deleting directories.

Mastering file and directory handling in PHP is a crucial skill, as it enables you to manage and interact with files on the server, an essential part of many web applications.

CHAPTER 11

SESSIONS AND COOKIES

Introduction to Sessions and Cookies

Sessions and **cookies** are two ways to store and manage user data in PHP. They allow you to track users and their activities across different pages, enabling a more dynamic and personalized web experience. While they both serve similar purposes, they work differently and have different uses.

1. **Sessions**:
   - A **session** is a way to store data on the server. It allows you to persist user data across multiple pages. Each user is assigned a unique session ID that is stored on the server. The session ID is sent to the user's browser as a cookie, and PHP uses this ID to retrieve session data on subsequent requests.
   - Sessions are ideal for storing sensitive information, such as user login credentials or preferences, because the data is stored on the server rather than in the user's browser.

2. **Cookies**:
   - A **cookie** is a small piece of data that is stored on the user's browser. Cookies are sent with each

129

HTTP request, allowing you to store and retrieve data for a specific user across different sessions.

o Cookies can be used for tracking user behavior, storing preferences, or remembering the user's login credentials (though sessions are preferred for sensitive information).

Storing Data in Sessions

To start using sessions in PHP, you need to begin the session with the `session_start()` function. This function must be called at the beginning of your PHP script to initialize the session and allow access to session variables.

1. **Starting a Session**:

   o The `session_start()` function starts the session, and you can then store and access session variables using the `$_SESSION` superglobal array.

Example:

php

```php
<?php
session_start();  // Start the session
```

```
// Store session data
$_SESSION['username'] = 'JohnDoe';
$_SESSION['loggedIn'] = true;

echo "Session data has been set!";
?>
```

2. **Accessing Session Data**:

   o   To access session variables, simply reference
       them from the $_SESSION array.

Example:

```
php

<?php
session_start();  // Start the session

// Check if session variable is set
if (isset($_SESSION['username'])) {
    echo "Hello, " . $_SESSION['username']
. "!";
} else {
    echo "No user is logged in.";
}
?>
```

3. **Destroying a Session**:

- o You can remove session data using `unset()` or destroy the entire session using `session_destroy()`.

Example:

```
php
```

```php
<?php
session_start();   // Start the session

// Unset session variable
unset($_SESSION['username']);

// Destroy the session
session_destroy();

echo "Session data cleared.";
?>
```

- o **Important**: `session_destroy()` does not immediately unset all session variables; it only marks the session for destruction. You must call `unset()` to remove specific session variables, and the session data will be cleaned up at the end of the script.

Setting and Accessing Cookies

Cookies are set using the `setcookie()` function, which allows you to send a small piece of data to the user's browser. Cookies can be set to expire after a certain time or when the browser is closed.

1. **Setting a Cookie**:
   o The `setcookie()` function takes several parameters:
      ▪ **Name**: The name of the cookie.
      ▪ **Value**: The value to store in the cookie.
      ▪ **Expiration**: The time when the cookie should expire (in Unix timestamp format).
      ▪ **Path**: The path on the server where the cookie is available.
      ▪ **Domain**: The domain where the cookie is available (optional).
      ▪ **Secure**: Whether the cookie should only be sent over HTTPS (optional).
      ▪ **HttpOnly**: Whether the cookie is only accessible via HTTP requests (optional).

   Example:

   ```
   php
   ```

133

```php
<?php
// Set a cookie that expires in 1 hour
setcookie("user", "JohnDoe", time() +
3600, "/");  // Cookie expires in 1 hour
echo "Cookie has been set!";
?>
```

- o In this example, the cookie named `user` is set with the value `JohnDoe` and will expire in 1 hour.

2. **Accessing Cookie Data**:
   - o After setting a cookie, you can access it through the `$_COOKIE` superglobal array.

Example:

php

```php
<?php
// Check if cookie is set
if (isset($_COOKIE['user'])) {
    echo "Welcome back, " .
$_COOKIE['user'] . "!";
} else {
    echo "No user cookie found.";
}
?>
```

3. **Deleting a Cookie**:

o   To delete a cookie, you can set its expiration date to a time in the past.

Example:

php

```php
<?php
// Delete the cookie by setting its
expiration to the past
setcookie("user", "", time() - 3600, "/");
echo "Cookie has been deleted.";
?>
```

Managing Session Security

When working with sessions, it's crucial to ensure that session data is handled securely, especially when dealing with sensitive information, such as user authentication details. Below are best practices for managing session security:

1. **Regenerating Session IDs**: To prevent session fixation attacks (where an attacker sets the session ID before the user logs in), you should regenerate the session ID whenever a new session is started, such as after a successful login.

Example:

```
php

<?php
session_start();  // Start the session

// Regenerate session ID to prevent session
fixation
session_regenerate_id(true);      // Pass
`true` to delete the old session

$_SESSION['username'] = 'JohnDoe';
echo "Session ID regenerated.";
?>
```

2. **Setting Secure Session Cookies**: To ensure that session cookies are only transmitted over HTTPS, you can set the `session.cookie_secure` and `session.cookie_httponly` options in the `php.ini` file or dynamically using `ini_set()`.

   o **`session.cookie_secure`**: Ensures cookies are only sent over HTTPS connections.

   o **`session.cookie_httponly`**: Prevents JavaScript from accessing the session cookie (helps prevent XSS attacks).

Example:

```
php
```

```php
<?php
// Set session cookie parameters for
security
ini_set('session.cookie_secure', 1);   //
Only send cookies over HTTPS
ini_set('session.cookie_httponly', 1);  //
Prevent JavaScript access to the cookie

session_start();
?>
```

3. **Session Timeout**: You can implement session timeout by checking the time of the last activity in the session. If the user is inactive for a certain period, you can destroy the session and require re-authentication.

   Example:

   ```
   php
   ```

   ```php
   <?php
   session_start();

   // Set session timeout (e.g., 15 minutes)
   $timeout_duration = 900;  // 15 minutes in
   seconds
   ```

137

```php
if (isset($_SESSION['last_activity']) &&
(time() - $_SESSION['last_activity']) >
$timeout_duration) {
    // Session has expired, destroy it
    session_unset();
    session_destroy();
    echo    "Session    expired    due    to
inactivity.";
} else {
    $_SESSION['last_activity']  =  time();
// Update the last activity time
}
?>
```

4. **Destroying Sessions Safely**: When you want to end a session, it's important to properly destroy both the session data and the session cookie to ensure that the session is fully terminated.

   Example:

```php
php

<?php
session_start();

// Clear session data
session_unset();
```

```php
// Destroy session cookie (if it's being
used)
if (ini_get("session.use_cookies")) {
    $params = session_get_cookie_params();
    setcookie(session_name(), '', time() -
42000, $params["path"], $params["domain"],
$params["secure"], $params["httponly"]);
}

// Destroy session
session_destroy();
echo "Session has been destroyed.";
?>
```

Summary

By the end of this chapter, you should be able to:

- Understand the differences between **sessions** and **cookies** and when to use each.
- Store and retrieve data in **sessions** using the $_SESSION superglobal array.
- Set, access, and delete **cookies** using the setcookie() function and the $_COOKIE superglobal.
- Implement security best practices for managing sessions, including session regeneration, timeout handling, and secure cookie settings.

Mastering sessions and cookies is essential for building secure and personalized web applications, as they allow you to track user interactions and store important data.

CHAPTER 12

INTRODUCTION TO MVC ARCHITECTURE

What is MVC (Model-View-Controller)?

MVC (Model-View-Controller) is a software architectural pattern that separates an application into three main components: **Model**, **View**, and **Controller**. This separation helps in organizing code in a way that makes it more manageable, scalable, and easier to maintain. MVC is widely used in web development frameworks to design dynamic web applications in an organized manner.

1. **Model**:
   o The **Model** represents the **data** and **business logic** of the application. It is responsible for handling the data, such as retrieving it from the database, processing it, and performing necessary operations (e.g., CRUD operations). The Model does not directly interact with the user interface but rather defines the structure of the data.
   o In PHP, the Model is typically responsible for interacting with the database (e.g., using MySQL queries, inserting, updating, or deleting records).

141

Example:

```
php
```

```php
class UserModel {
    public function getUserById($id) {
        // Example database query to
retrieve a user
        return "SELECT * FROM users WHERE
id = $id";
    }
}
```

2. **View**:

   o The **View** is responsible for presenting the data to the user. It represents the user interface (UI) and is responsible for rendering the content that the user sees and interacts with. The View is **separated from the business logic** and doesn't process any data directly.

   o In PHP, Views are typically HTML files (with embedded PHP for dynamic content) that display the data retrieved from the Model.

Example:

```
php
```

```php
class UserView {
```

142

```
public function render($userData) {
    echo      "User      Name:      "      .
$userData['name'] . "<br>";
    echo      "User      Email:      "      .
$userData['email'] . "<br>";
    }
}
```

3. **Controller**:

- o The **Controller** acts as an intermediary between the Model and the View. It takes user input (e.g., from a form or URL request), processes it, interacts with the Model to retrieve or update data, and then updates the View to reflect the changes.

- o The Controller **handles user requests**, decides which actions need to be taken based on the input, and then updates the appropriate Model and View.

Example:

php

```
class UserController {
    public function showUser($id) {
        $model = new UserModel();
        $view = new UserView();
```

143

```
// Get data from model
$userData              =              $model-
>getUserById($id);

// Render data with view
$view->render($userData);
    }
}
```

In summary:

- The **Model** handles data and business logic.
- The **View** displays data to the user and manages the UI.
- The **Controller** handles user input, manipulates data through the Model, and updates the View.

Benefits of Using MVC in Web Development

Using the **MVC** architecture offers several benefits that can greatly improve the organization, maintainability, and scalability of your web applications:

1. **Separation of Concerns**:
   - The core benefit of MVC is the **separation of concerns**, where the data (Model), user interface (View), and control logic (Controller) are kept separate. This makes the codebase more

organized and easier to manage. Developers can work on different components independently without interfering with each other's work.

2. **Maintainability**:
   o Since the logic for handling data is separate from the presentation (View), it is easier to update or fix bugs in any part of the application without affecting others. For example, you can change how data is displayed in the View without altering the data handling in the Model.

3. **Scalability**:
   o MVC allows for **scalability** by isolating the components. As your application grows, it becomes easier to add new features. You can add more Controllers for handling new routes, more Models for managing new data, and Views for displaying new pages without disrupting existing functionality.

4. **Testability**:
   o The MVC pattern encourages testing individual components. For example, the Model can be unit-tested without worrying about the user interface. Similarly, Views can be tested separately from business logic. This makes it easier to implement automated testing and ensures high-quality code.

5. **Code Reusability**:

145

- o Since the Controller handles the communication between the Model and View, and the View is separate from the business logic, developers can **reuse the same View** to display different types of data. Similarly, the same data handling logic in the Model can be reused across different pages or user actions.

6. **Improved Collaboration**:

- o MVC promotes **collaboration** between front-end and back-end developers. The separation of the View and Controller allows front-end developers to focus on the UI, while back-end developers can concentrate on the business logic and data processing. Both teams can work on the project simultaneously without interfering with each other.

Structure of an MVC-Based PHP Application

An MVC-based PHP application typically follows a specific folder structure to organize the Model, View, and Controller components. Below is a basic structure of a PHP application that follows the MVC pattern:

arduino

```
/myapp
    /app
        /controllers        // Contains Controller
classes
            UserController.php
            ProductController.php
        /models                 // Contains Model
classes
            UserModel.php
            ProductModel.php
        /views              // Contains View files
(HTML + PHP)
            user_view.php
            product_view.php
    /public
        index.php           // Entry point of the
application
    /config
        config.php          // Configuration files
    /core
        Router.php          // Handles URL routing
        Controller.php      // Base controller class
        Model.php           // Base model class
```

1. **Controllers Folder**:

    o This folder contains the classes responsible for handling user requests and calling the appropriate methods on the Model and View. For example, UserController.php could handle displaying

147

a user's profile and interacting with the
`UserModel`.

2. **Models Folder**:

   o This folder contains the classes that interact with
   the database and perform business logic. Each
   model class represents a specific resource (e.g.,
   User, Product) and contains methods to retrieve,
   insert, update, or delete data from the database.

3. **Views Folder**:

   o This folder contains the files responsible for
   displaying data to the user. Views are typically
   HTML files with embedded PHP to display
   dynamic content, such as user details, product
   information, etc.

4. **Public Folder**:

   o The `index.php` file in this folder acts as the
   entry point of the application. All requests from
   the user are routed to `index.php`, which then
   passes them to the appropriate Controller.

5. **Config Folder**:

   o The `config.php` file contains configuration
   settings for the application, such as database
   credentials, environment settings, etc.

6. **Core Folder**:

   o The core classes handle fundamental tasks, such
   as routing and initializing models and views. For

example, `Router.php` handles routing requests to the appropriate controllers, and `Controller.php` serves as a base class for all controller classes.

Example of MVC Flow in PHP

1. **URL Request**:
   o A user visits the URL `http://example.com/user/1`. The router in `index.php` determines that the `UserController` class and the `show` method should be called.
2. **Controller**:
   o `UserController.php` processes the request and calls the `UserModel` to retrieve data for the user with ID 1.
3. **Model**:
   o `UserModel.php` fetches the data from the database and returns it to the controller.
4. **View**:
   o The controller passes the data to `user_view.php`, which is responsible for displaying the user's profile in the browser.

149

Summary

By the end of this chapter, you should be able to:

- Understand the core concepts of **MVC (Model-View-Controller)** and how they relate to web development.
- Appreciate the **benefits** of using MVC, including separation of concerns, maintainability, and scalability.
- Recognize the typical **structure** of an MVC-based PHP application, including how Controllers, Models, and Views work together.

Mastering the MVC architecture will allow you to build clean, scalable, and maintainable PHP applications, separating business logic, presentation, and data management in a way that simplifies development and enhances collaboration.

CHAPTER 13

BUILDING YOUR FIRST PHP WEB APPLICATION (PART 1)

Project Planning and Design

Before diving into writing code, it's essential to plan and design your PHP web application. This phase involves defining the application's requirements, outlining its functionality, and determining how the different parts of the application will work together. Proper planning will ensure that the development process is smooth and organized.

1. **Define the Purpose of the Application**:
    o   What problem does the application solve?
    o   Who will use the application, and what are their needs?
    o   For example, a simple blog system where users can view, add, edit, and delete posts.

2. **Outline the Features**:
    o   Create a list of the features your application will have. For example:
        - **Users**: Register, log in, and log out.
        - **Posts**: Create, read, update, and delete posts.

151

- **Comments**: Allow users to comment on posts.
  - ○ Break these features into smaller, manageable tasks.

3. **Wireframing and UI Design**:
   - ○ Sketch out the user interface (UI) to visualize how the application will look.
   - ○ Design wireframes for each page (e.g., homepage, post creation page, user dashboard).
   - ○ Focus on the user experience (UX) by planning easy navigation and user-friendly forms.

4. **Technology Stack**:
   - ○ Decide on the technologies you'll use. For this PHP web application, we'll use:
     - **Frontend**: HTML, CSS (for styling), and optionally, JavaScript for dynamic interactions.
     - **Backend**: PHP (for server-side scripting) and MySQL (for the database).
     - **Folder Structure**: We'll follow the Model-View-Controller (MVC) pattern for better code organization.

Setting Up Your Project Structure

A clean, well-organized project structure is critical for scaling and maintaining the application as it grows. Let's set up a simple MVC-based folder structure.

1. **Directory Structure**: Here's an example folder structure for the application:

```
arduino

/myapp
    /app
        /controllers        //   Contains
Controller classes
            PostController.php
            UserController.php
        /models        // Contains Model
classes
            PostModel.php
            UserModel.php
        /views        // Contains View
files (HTML + PHP)
            header.php
            footer.php
            home.php
            post.php
    /public
```

```
        index.php       // Entry point of
the application
    /config
        config.php        // Configuration
file for database connection
    /core
        Router.php      // Handles routing
requests
        Controller.php // Base controller
class
        Model.php       // Base model class
```

2. **Explanation of Folders**:
   - **/app/controllers**: Stores the controllers that handle user requests and interact with models to retrieve data.
   - **/app/models**: Contains the model classes that interact with the database and manage the data.
   - **/app/views**: Holds the views (HTML templates) that display the content to the user.
   - **/public**: The index.php file is the entry point to the application. It receives all incoming requests and routes them accordingly.
   - **/config**: Contains configuration files, such as database connection settings.
   - **/core**: Contains core classes like the Router, which directs requests to the appropriate

controller, and the base classes for Models and Controllers.

Creating the Database and Defining Models

Now that we have our basic project structure, the next step is to create the database and define the models.

1. **Database Design**: For a blog application, we need a few basic tables:

    o **Users**: Stores user information (name, email, password).

    o **Posts**: Stores blog posts (title, content, author, date).

    o **Comments**: Stores comments on posts (user_id, post_id, content, date).

    Here's an example SQL script to create these tables:

```sql
sql

CREATE DATABASE blog;

USE blog;

-- Create Users table
CREATE TABLE users (
```

```
    id INT AUTO_INCREMENT PRIMARY KEY,
    name VARCHAR(100) NOT NULL,
    email VARCHAR(100) NOT NULL UNIQUE,
    password VARCHAR(255) NOT NULL
);


-- Create Posts table
CREATE TABLE posts (
    id INT AUTO_INCREMENT PRIMARY KEY,
    title VARCHAR(255) NOT NULL,
    content TEXT NOT NULL,
    user_id INT,
    created_at        TIMESTAMP        DEFAULT
CURRENT_TIMESTAMP,
    FOREIGN   KEY   (user_id)   REFERENCES
users(id)
);


-- Create Comments table
CREATE TABLE comments (
    id INT AUTO_INCREMENT PRIMARY KEY,
    user_id INT,
    post_id INT,
    content TEXT NOT NULL,
    created_at        TIMESTAMP        DEFAULT
CURRENT_TIMESTAMP,
    FOREIGN   KEY   (user_id)   REFERENCES
users(id),
```

```
FOREIGN    KEY    (post_id)    REFERENCES
posts(id)
);
```

2. **Defining the Model for Users and Posts**: Once the database is created, define models to interact with the database and handle data.

Example: UserModel:

php

```php
<?php
class UserModel {
    private $db;

    public function __construct($db) {
        $this->db = $db;
    }

    public function getUserByEmail($email) {
        $query = "SELECT * FROM users WHERE email = :email";
        $stmt = $this->db->prepare($query);
        $stmt->bindParam(':email', $email);
        $stmt->execute();
        return $stmt->fetch();
```

```
        }

    public    function    createUser($name,
$email, $password) {
        $query = "INSERT INTO users (name,
email,  password) VALUES  (:name,  :email,
:password)";
        $stmt           =           $this->db-
>prepare($query);
        $stmt->bindParam(':name', $name);
        $stmt->bindParam(':email',
$email);
        $stmt->bindParam(':password',
password_hash($password,
PASSWORD_DEFAULT));
        return $stmt->execute();
    }
}
```

Example: PostModel:

php

```php
<?php
class PostModel {
    private $db;

    public function __construct($db) {
        $this->db = $db;
    }
```

158

```
public function getAllPosts() {
    $query = "SELECT * FROM posts ORDER
BY created_at DESC";
    $stmt = $this->db->query($query);
    return $stmt->fetchAll();
}


public function createPost($title,
$content, $userId) {
    $query = "INSERT INTO posts (title,
content, user_id) VALUES (:title,
:content, :user_id)";
    $stmt = $this->db-
>prepare($query);
    $stmt->bindParam(':title',
$title);
    $stmt->bindParam(':content',
$content);
    $stmt->bindParam(':user_id',
$userId);
    return $stmt->execute();
}
}
```

3. **Database Connection**: In the `config` folder, create a `config.php` file to handle the database connection. For simplicity, we'll use **PDO** (PHP Data Objects) for database interaction.

config.php:

php

```php
<?php
$host = 'localhost';
$dbname = 'blog';
$username = 'root';
$password = '';

try {
    $db                           = new
PDO("mysql:host=$host;dbname=$dbname",
$username, $password);
    $db->setAttribute(PDO::ATTR_ERRMODE,
PDO::ERRMODE_EXCEPTION);
} catch (PDOException $e) {
    echo "Connection failed: " . $e-
>getMessage();
}
?>
```

Building Views with HTML and PHP

The **View** component in the MVC architecture handles the display of data to the user. In this section, we will create views to display blog posts and a form to create new posts.

1. **Home View (Displaying All Posts)**: The home.php view will display a list of all blog posts.

   home.php:

   php

```php
<?php
// Include the header
include('views/header.php');
?>

<h1>All Posts</h1>

<?php foreach ($posts as $post): ?>
    <div class="post">
        <h2><?php echo $post['title']; ?></h2>
        <p><?php echo substr($post['content'], 0, 100); ?>...</p>
        <a href="post.php?id=<?php echo $post['id']; ?>">Read more</a>
    </div>
<?php endforeach; ?>

<?php
// Include the footer
include('views/footer.php');
```

161

```
?>
```

2. **Post View (Displaying a Single Post)**: The `post.php` view will display a single post in detail.

   post.php:

   php

   ```php
   <?php
   include('views/header.php');
   ?>

   <h1><?php echo $post['title']; ?></h1>
   <p><?php echo $post['content']; ?></p>
   <p>Posted by: <?php echo $author['name'];
   ?></p>

   <?php
   include('views/footer.php');
   ?>
   ```

3. **Form for Creating a Post**: We will also need a form to create a new post. This form will be displayed in the `create.php` view.

   create.php:

   php

```php
<?php
include('views/header.php');
?>


<h1>Create New Post</h1>

<form            action="create_post.php"
method="POST">
    <label for="title">Title</label>
    <input    type="text"    id="title"
name="title" required><br><br>

    <label for="content">Content</label>
    <textarea id="content" name="content"
required></textarea><br><br>

    <button        type="submit">Create
Post</button>
</form>

<?php
include('views/footer.php');
?>
```

Summary

By the end of this chapter, you should be able to:

- **Plan** and design a simple PHP web application.
- Set up a **project structure** using the MVC pattern.
- Create a **database** with tables for users, posts, and comments, and define corresponding **models** to interact with the database.
- Build **views** to display data and handle user input using HTML and PHP.

This is just the first part of building a PHP web application, setting the foundation for dynamic content management. In the next chapter, you will learn how to integrate controllers to handle user input and manage the application's flow.

CHAPTER 14

BUILDING YOUR FIRST PHP
WEB APPLICATION (PART 2)

Implementing Controllers and Routing

In Part 1 of this chapter, we set up the basic structure of a PHP web application using the MVC pattern. Now, in Part 2, we'll focus on implementing **controllers** and **routing** to handle user requests and process them accordingly.

1. **What is Routing?**
   Routing refers to mapping incoming requests (usually URLs) to specific controller actions. It helps direct traffic to the appropriate function within the application. A routing mechanism interprets the URL, processes it, and calls the relevant controller to handle the request.

2. **Creating the Router Class**:
   The router class will map URLs to controller methods. We can create a `Router.php` file in the `core` folder.

Example: Router.php:

```
php
```

```php
<?php
```

```php
class Router {
    private $routes = [];

    // Add route
    public         function         add($route,
$controller, $action) {
        $this->routes[$route]              =
['controller' => $controller, 'action' =>
$action];
    }

    // Dispatch the request
    public function dispatch($url) {
        foreach ($this->routes as $route
=> $controllerAction) {
            if ($url == $route) {
                $controllerName          =
$controllerAction['controller'];
                $action                  =
$controllerAction['action'];
                $controller     =     new
$controllerName();
                $controller->$action();
                return;
            }
        }
        echo "Route not found!";
    }
}
```

?>

3. **Adding Routes**: In the index.php file (located in the public directory), instantiate the Router class and add routes.

Example: index.php:

php

```php
<?php
// Include the required files
require_once '../config/config.php';
require_once '../core/Router.php';
require_once
'../app/controllers/PostController.php';

$router = new Router();
$router->add('/home',    'PostController',
'index');
$router->add('/post',    'PostController',
'show');

$url = $_SERVER['REQUEST_URI'];  // Get the
URL from the browser
$router->dispatch($url);  // Dispatch the
URL to the correct controller
?>
```

167

4. **Controller Example**: The controller defines how to process the data and respond to the user's request. The controller's job is to interact with the model, fetch data, and pass it to the view.

Example: PostController.php:

php

```php
<?php
class PostController {
    public function index() {
        // Retrieve all posts from the model
        $model = new PostModel();
        $posts = $model->getAllPosts();

        // Display posts in the view
        include '../app/views/home.php';
    }

    public function show() {
        // Retrieve a single post from the model
        $id = $_GET['id'];
        $model = new PostModel();
        $post = $model->getPostById($id);

        // Display post in the view
```

```
                include '../app/views/post.php';
    }
}
?>
```

Handling User Authentication and Authorization

User authentication and authorization are critical components of most web applications. Authentication ensures that users are who they claim to be, while authorization determines whether a user has permission to perform a specific action.

1. **User Authentication**: Authentication typically involves verifying a user's identity through a **login** process. After successful login, the user's credentials are stored in the session, so they don't need to log in again until the session expires.

   Login Form (View):

   php

   ```
   <!-- login.php -->
   <form action="login.php" method="POST">
       <label for="email">Email:</label>
       <input    type="email"    id="email"
   name="email" required>
   ```

```
    <label
for="password">Password:</label>
    <input type="password" id="password"
name="password" required>
    <button type="submit">Login</button>
</form>
```

2. **Handling Login (Controller)**:

   o In the controller, you can process the user's credentials by checking them against the database. If valid, you start a session and store the user's information.

   Example: login.php (Controller):

   php

```php
<?php
session_start();
require_once 'UserModel.php';

if ($_SERVER['REQUEST_METHOD'] == 'POST')
{
    $email = $_POST['email'];
    $password = $_POST['password'];

    $userModel = new UserModel();
    $user           =           $userModel-
>getUserByEmail($email);
```

```php
    // Check if user exists and password is
correct
    if              ($user              &&
password_verify($password,
$user['password'])) {
        $_SESSION['user_id']              =
$user['id'];
        $_SESSION['username']             =
$user['name'];
        header('Location: home.php');
    } else {
        echo "Invalid email or password!";
    }
}
?>
```

3. **Authorization**: Once a user is authenticated, you may
   need to check if they are authorized to access specific
   content or perform certain actions (e.g., admin
   privileges).

   Example: Check User Role (Controller):

```php
php

<?php
session_start();
```

```php
// Check if the user is logged in and is an
admin
if    (!isset($_SESSION['user_id'])      ||
$_SESSION['role'] !== 'admin') {
    header('Location: login.php');
    exit();
}

// Admin-specific content
echo "Welcome, Admin!";
?>
```

Introduction to Form Validation and Error Handling

Form validation ensures that the user inputs the correct data. It's important to validate form data on both the client-side (using JavaScript) and server-side (using PHP) to ensure the data is accurate, complete, and secure.

1. **Server-side Form Validation**: Server-side validation occurs after the form is submitted. You check if the submitted data meets certain criteria (e.g., required fields, correct format) and return errors if the validation fails.

    Example: Register.php (Controller):

    php

172

```php
<?php
if ($_SERVER["REQUEST_METHOD"] == "POST")
{
    $name = $_POST['name'];
    $email = $_POST['email'];
    $password = $_POST['password'];

    $errors = [];

    // Validate Name
    if (empty($name)) {
        $errors[] = "Name is required.";
    }

    // Validate Email
    if          (empty($email)          ||
!filter_var($email,
FILTER_VALIDATE_EMAIL)) {
        $errors[]   =   "Valid   email   is
required.";
    }

    // Validate Password
    if          (empty($password)          ||
strlen($password) < 6) {
        $errors[] = "Password must be at
least 6 characters long.";
    }
```

173

```php
    // Display errors or process the form
    if (empty($errors)) {
        // Proceed with registration
(e.g., insert into database)
        echo "Form submitted
successfully!";
    } else {
        foreach ($errors as $error) {
            echo "<p>$error</p>";
        }
    }
}
?>
```

2. **Displaying Form Errors**: If validation fails, it's important to provide feedback to the user. You can display the errors above or below the form fields.

Example: HTML Form with Error Display:

php

```php
<form action="register.php" method="POST">
    <label for="name">Name:</label>
    <input type="text" id="name"
name="name" value="<?php echo $name; ?>">
    <span><?php echo $errors['name'] ??
''; ?></span><br>

    <label for="email">Email:</label>
```

174

```
    <input    type="email"    id="email"
name="email"  value="<?php  echo  $email;
?>">
    <span><?php echo $errors['email'] ??
''; ?></span><br>

    <label
for="password">Password:</label>
    <input  type="password"  id="password"
name="password">
    <span><?php  echo  $errors['password']
?? ''; ?></span><br>

    <button
type="submit">Register</button>
</form>
```

3. **Error Handling**: Error handling in PHP allows you to capture and handle exceptions or warnings that might occur during script execution.

   Basic Error Handling:

   php

```
<?php
try {
    // Some code that may throw an
exception
```

```
    throw    new    Exception("An    error
occurred!");
} catch (Exception $e) {
    echo  "Caught  exception:  "  .  $e-
>getMessage();    // Display  the  error
message
}
?>
```

o **Error Logging**: You can log errors to a file using `error_log()` for debugging purposes.

Example:

php

```php
<?php
if ($_SERVER["REQUEST_METHOD"] == "POST")
{
    $name = $_POST['name'];

    // Log an error if name is empty
    if (empty($name)) {
        error_log("Name is required at " .
date("Y-m-d H:i:s"));
        echo "Please provide your name.";
    }
}
?>
```

Summary

By the end of this chapter, you should be able to:

- Implement **controllers** and **routing** to handle user requests and map them to appropriate actions.
- Handle **user authentication** by creating login forms and verifying user credentials.
- Implement **authorization** to restrict access based on user roles (e.g., admin access).
- Validate form data on the **server-side** and display **validation errors** for users.
- Handle **errors and exceptions** gracefully in your application.

With these features, you are well on your way to building dynamic, user-friendly web applications in PHP. In the next chapter, you will learn how to enhance your application further with advanced features like database interaction, CRUD operations, and more.

CHAPTER 15

INTEGRATING PHP WITH FRONT-END TECHNOLOGIES

Using PHP with HTML, CSS, and JavaScript

PHP is a server-side scripting language, while HTML, CSS, and JavaScript are primarily used on the client-side. However, PHP can be used to dynamically generate HTML content, embed CSS styles, and interact with JavaScript, creating a seamless integration between server-side and client-side technologies.

1. **Embedding PHP in HTML**: PHP can be embedded directly into HTML files using `<?php ... ?>` tags. This allows you to dynamically insert data or logic into an HTML page. PHP is processed on the server before the HTML is sent to the browser.

Example: Embedding PHP in HTML:

```
php
```

```
<!DOCTYPE html>
<html>
<head>
    <title>Welcome to My Website</title>
```

```
<style>
    body { font-family: Arial, sans-
serif; }
    h1 { color: blue; }
</style>
</head>
<body>
    <h1>Welcome to <?php echo "My Awesome
Website!"; ?></h1>
    <p>Today's date is: <?php echo date("Y-
m-d"); ?></p>
</body>
</html>
```

- o In this example, PHP is used to generate dynamic content such as the website title and the current date.

2. **PHP and CSS**: You can use PHP to dynamically generate CSS styles based on user preferences or other dynamic conditions. For example, you can create a dynamic theme for your website where users can choose a color scheme.

Example: Dynamic CSS with PHP:

```php
php

<?php
$bgColor = "lightblue"; // This could be
dynamically set based on user preferences
```

179

```
?>
<style>
    body {
        background-color:    <?php    echo
$bgColor; ?>;
    }
</style>
```

3. **PHP and JavaScript**: PHP can be used to pass data to JavaScript. This is particularly useful when you need to generate dynamic JavaScript code or pass server-side data to the client-side for use in interactive features (e.g., AJAX).

   Example: PHP to JavaScript:

   php

```
<?php
$userName = "John Doe";
?>
<script>
    var userName = "<?php echo $userName;
?>"; // Pass PHP variable to JavaScript
    alert("Hello, " + userName);    //
Outputs: Hello, John Doe
</script>
```

o In this example, the PHP variable `$userName` is passed to the JavaScript variable `userName`, and JavaScript uses it to display a personalized message.

Introduction to Templating Engines (e.g., Twig)

Templating engines are tools that separate the logic of PHP from the presentation (HTML). A templating engine allows you to write cleaner, more maintainable code by using templates for the views (the frontend of the application), while keeping business logic (PHP) separate.

1. **What is a Templating Engine?** A **templating engine** is a tool that allows you to generate dynamic HTML content by using templates, which include placeholders for data that is dynamically inserted during runtime. This helps to keep the code for rendering the views clean and organized.

2. **Benefits of Using a Templating Engine**:
   o **Separation of Concerns**: By separating PHP logic from HTML presentation, the code becomes easier to maintain and understand.
   o **Reusability**: Templates can be reused across different parts of the application, reducing redundancy.

181

- o **Security**: Templating engines often provide built-in protection against cross-site scripting (XSS) by escaping data automatically.

3. **Twig Templating Engine**: **Twig** is a popular templating engine for PHP. It allows you to write clean and readable templates with easy-to-understand syntax and powerful features.

  - o **Installation**: If you're using Composer (PHP's dependency manager), you can install Twig like this:

```bash
composer require "twig/twig:^3.0"
```

  - o **Using Twig**: Once Twig is installed, you can integrate it into your PHP application.

  Example: Basic Twig Setup:

```php
// Load Composer's autoloader
require_once '/path/to/vendor/autoload.php';

// Set up Twig
```

182

```
$loader            =            new
\Twig\Loader\FilesystemLoader('path
/to/templates');
$twig              =            new
\Twig\Environment($loader);

// Render a template
echo      $twig->render('index.html',
['name' => 'John Doe']);
```

o **Creating a Template (index.html)**: In the templates directory, create a template file (index.html).

```
html
```

```
<html>
<body>
    <h1>Hello, {{ name }}!</h1>
</body>
</html>
```

o In this example, {{ name }} is a placeholder that will be replaced with the value passed from PHP when rendering the template.

4. **Twig Syntax**:

o **Variables**: Variables are enclosed in {{ }}.

o **Control Structures**: You can use {% %} for loops and conditions.

183

Example with Loop and Condition:

php

```
// Controller
$posts = [
    ['title' => 'First Post', 'author' =>
'John'],
    ['title' => 'Second Post', 'author' =>
'Sarah'],
];
echo $twig->render('posts.html', ['posts'
=> $posts]);
```

posts.html (Template):

html

```
<ul>
{% for post in posts %}
    <li>{{ post.title }} by {{ post.author
}}</li>
{% else %}
    <li>No posts available</li>
{% endfor %}
</ul>
```

- o **Output**:

    html

184

```
<ul>
    <li>First Post by John</li>
    <li>Second Post by Sarah</li>
</ul>
```

Dynamic Content Rendering with PHP

PHP allows you to render dynamic content based on user input, database queries, or any other server-side logic. Rendering dynamic content enables you to create interactive and personalized websites that respond to the user.

1. **Dynamic Content with PHP**: PHP can generate dynamic HTML content by embedding PHP code directly into the HTML page. For example, you might display the user's name or other personalized data.

    Example: Displaying User Data:

    php

```php
<?php
// Assume we have user data stored in the
session or database
session_start();
$_SESSION['username'] = "John Doe";
?>
```

```
<html>
<body>
    <h1>Welcome,          <?php          echo
$_SESSION['username']; ?>!</h1>
</body>
</html>
```

- o **Explanation**: In this example, PHP dynamically displays the user's name on the page by inserting the value of $_SESSION['username'] directly into the HTML.

2. **Rendering Data from the Database**: PHP is commonly used to query a database (e.g., MySQL) and dynamically generate HTML content based on the data retrieved.

Example: Displaying Posts from a Database:

php

```php
<?php
// Assume we have a connection to the
database and query for posts
$pdo                  =                  new
PDO('mysql:host=localhost;dbname=myapp',
'root', '');
$stmt = $pdo->query('SELECT title, content
FROM posts');
$posts = $stmt->fetchAll();
?>
```

186

```
<html>
<body>
    <h1>All Posts</h1>
    <ul>
    <?php foreach ($posts as $post): ?>
        <li>
            <h2><?php                    echo
htmlspecialchars($post['title']); ?></h2>
            <p><?php                     echo
htmlspecialchars($post['content']); ?></p>
        </li>
    <?php endforeach; ?>
    </ul>
</body>
</html>
```

- o **Explanation**: In this example, PHP queries the
  database for all posts, then loops through the
  results to display each post's title and content. We
  use `htmlspecialchars()` to prevent XSS
  attacks by escaping any special HTML characters
  in the output.

3. **Handling Form Data**: PHP is often used to process form
   submissions, validate the data, and display feedback to the
   user. You can render dynamic content based on the form
   input.

Example: Handling Form Submission:

```
php

<?php
if ($_SERVER['REQUEST_METHOD'] == 'POST')
{
    $username = $_POST['username'];
    echo          "Welcome,          "          .
htmlspecialchars($username) . "!";
}
?>
<form action="" method="POST">
    <label          for="username">Username:
</label>
    <input    type="text"    name="username"
id="username">
    <button type="submit">Submit</button>
</form>
```

- o **Explanation**: This form submits the user's username, and PHP processes the input to display a personalized greeting. The `htmlspecialchars()` function is used to avoid XSS vulnerabilities

Summary

By the end of this chapter, you should be able to:

- Integrate **PHP** with **HTML**, **CSS**, and **JavaScript** to create dynamic, interactive web pages.
- Use a **templating engine** like **Twig** to separate PHP logic from presentation and generate dynamic content more efficiently.
- Render **dynamic content** by interacting with databases, processing form data, and generating HTML output based on user input or server-side logic.

Integrating PHP with front-end technologies allows you to create rich, interactive, and dynamic web applications. Templating engines like Twig provide a more structured and cleaner way to handle dynamic content while keeping the codebase organized and maintainable.

189

CHAPTER 16

WORKING WITH APIS IN PHP

Understanding APIs (RESTful and SOAP)

APIs (Application Programming Interfaces) are a way for different software applications to communicate with each other. They allow you to send and receive data in a structured way. There are two main types of APIs used in web development:

1. **RESTful APIs**:

    o **REST (Representational State Transfer)** is an architectural style for designing networked applications. RESTful APIs use HTTP requests to interact with data and typically communicate in a stateless manner.

    o REST APIs are based on standard HTTP methods (GET, POST, PUT, DELETE) and often return data in **JSON** or **XML** format.

    o RESTful APIs are lightweight, easy to understand, and commonly used for web services, making them popular for modern web and mobile applications.

Key Features of RESTful APIs:

- o Uses standard HTTP methods:
  - **GET**: Retrieve data.
  - **POST**: Create new data.
  - **PUT**: Update existing data.
  - **DELETE**: Delete data.
- o Communicates using lightweight formats such as **JSON** and **XML**.
- o Stateless: Each request from the client contains all the information the server needs to process it.

Example of a RESTful API Request:

- o URL: `https://api.example.com/posts`
  - **GET**: Retrieve all posts.
  - **POST**: Create a new post.
  - **PUT**: Update an existing post.
  - **DELETE**: Delete a post.

2. **SOAP APIs**:

- o **SOAP (Simple Object Access Protocol)** is a protocol for exchanging structured information in the implementation of web services. SOAP APIs are more rigid compared to RESTful APIs and use **XML** for data exchange.
- o SOAP APIs tend to be more complex and are often used in enterprise applications.

Key Features of SOAP APIs:

- o Uses XML for data exchange.
- o Operates over multiple protocols (HTTP, SMTP, etc.).
- o Provides greater security and built-in error handling.
- o Requires a more strict structure (e.g., WSDL - Web Service Definition Language).

Example of a SOAP API Request:

- o URL: `https://api.example.com/soap`
  - The request involves sending an XML envelope, often with headers and parameters.

For most modern web applications, **RESTful APIs** are preferred due to their simplicity and flexibility.

Sending and Receiving Data with cURL

cURL (Client URL) is a powerful library in PHP that allows you to make HTTP requests to interact with APIs. It supports various protocols such as HTTP, HTTPS, FTP, and more.

1. **Sending Data with cURL**: cURL allows you to send HTTP requests to external APIs. You can send **GET**,

POST, **PUT**, or **DELETE** requests with it. Let's start with a basic **GET** request.

Example: Sending a GET Request with cURL:

php

```php
<?php
$url = "https://api.example.com/posts";

// Initialize cURL session
$ch = curl_init();

// Set the URL and other options
curl_setopt($ch, CURLOPT_URL, $url);
curl_setopt($ch,   CURLOPT_RETURNTRANSFER,
true);   // Return response as a string

// Execute cURL request and get the
response
$response = curl_exec($ch);

// Check for errors
if ($response === false) {
    echo "cURL Error: " . curl_error($ch);
} else {
    // Decode JSON response
    $data = json_decode($response, true);
```

```
        print_r($data);    // Output the data
from the API
}


// Close the cURL session
curl_close($ch);
?>
```

Explanation:

- o `curl_init()` initializes a new cURL session.
- o `curl_setopt()` is used to set various cURL options such as the request URL and return transfer settings.
- o `curl_exec()` executes the request and retrieves the response.
- o `curl_close()` closes the cURL session.

2. **Sending a POST Request with cURL**: In addition to sending **GET** requests, you can use **POST** requests to send data to an API. You can send form data, JSON data, or other types of content.

Example: Sending Data with a POST Request:

```
php

<?php
$url = "https://api.example.com/posts";
$data = [
```

```php
    'title' => 'New Post',
    'content' => 'This is a new blog post.'
];

// Initialize cURL session
$ch = curl_init();

// Set cURL options for POST request
curl_setopt($ch, CURLOPT_URL, $url);
curl_setopt($ch,   CURLOPT_RETURNTRANSFER,
true);  // Return response as a string
curl_setopt($ch, CURLOPT_POST, true);  //
Set POST method
curl_setopt($ch,       CURLOPT_POSTFIELDS,
http_build_query($data));  // Send data as
URL-encoded

// Execute the POST request
$response = curl_exec($ch);

// Check for errors
if ($response === false) {
    echo "cURL Error: " . curl_error($ch);
} else {
    // Process the response
    echo "Response: " . $response;
}

// Close the cURL session
```

```
curl_close($ch);
?>
```

Explanation:

- o `curl_setopt($ch, CURLOPT_POST, true)` sets the HTTP request method to **POST**.
- o `curl_setopt($ch, CURLOPT_POSTFIELDS, http_build_query($data))` sends the form data (e.g., title and content).
- o The response can be processed based on the API's return format.

Creating a Simple API with PHP

Now that we've learned how to interact with APIs, let's build a simple RESTful API using PHP. We'll create an API that handles basic CRUD operations (Create, Read, Update, Delete) for blog posts.

1. **Setting Up the API**: For simplicity, we'll store the posts in a simple array instead of a database.

    Example: Simple API (index.php):

    ```
    php
    ```

    ```
    <?php
    ```

```php
// Sample data (posts)
$posts = [
    1 => ['title' => 'First Post',
'content' => 'This is the first post.'],
    2 => ['title' => 'Second Post',
'content' => 'This is the second post.']
];

// Handle the request
header('Content-Type: application/json');

// Get the HTTP method and requested
resource
$method = $_SERVER['REQUEST_METHOD'];
$uri          =          explode('/',
trim($_SERVER['REQUEST_URI'], '/'));

// Check if the API is accessing the posts
resource
if ($uri[0] === 'posts') {
    if ($method === 'GET') {
        // Retrieve all posts or a single
post
        if (isset($uri[1])) {
            $id = (int) $uri[1];
            if (isset($posts[$id])) {
                echo
json_encode($posts[$id]);
            } else {
```

```php
                echo  json_encode(['error'
=> 'Post not found']);
            }
        } else {
            echo json_encode($posts);
        }
    } elseif ($method === 'POST') {
        // Add a new post
        $data                          =
json_decode(file_get_contents('php://inpu
t'), true);
        $id = count($posts) + 1;
        $posts[$id] = $data;
        echo   json_encode(['success'   =>
'Post added', 'id' => $id]);
    } elseif ($method === 'PUT') {
        // Update an existing post
        $id = (int) $uri[1];
        if (isset($posts[$id])) {
            $data                        =
json_decode(file_get_contents('php://inpu
t'), true);
            $posts[$id] = $data;
            echo json_encode(['success' =>
'Post updated']);
        } else {
            echo  json_encode(['error'  =>
'Post not found']);
        }
```

```
} elseif ($method === 'DELETE') {
    // Delete a post
    $id = (int) $uri[1];
    if (isset($posts[$id])) {
        unset($posts[$id]);
        echo json_encode(['success' =>
'Post deleted']);
    } else {
        echo json_encode(['error' =>
'Post not found']);
    }
}
} else {
    echo json_encode(['error' => 'Invalid
API endpoint']);
}
?>
```

Explanation:

o   This simple PHP script handles **GET, POST, PUT,** and **DELETE** methods for a posts resource.

o   It accepts requests like:

- GET /posts: Get all posts.
- GET /posts/1: Get the post with ID 1.
- POST /posts: Create a new post.
- PUT /posts/1: Update the post with ID 1.

199

- DELETE /posts/1: Delete the post with ID 1.

Consuming Third-Party APIs in PHP

To consume third-party APIs, you can use PHP to make requests to external APIs and retrieve their data. This allows you to integrate data from other services into your PHP application.

1. **Using cURL to Consume a Third-Party API**: Let's consume a public API (for example, the **JSONPlaceholder** API, a free fake online REST API for testing and prototyping).

   Example: Fetching Posts from JSONPlaceholder:

   php

```php
<?php
$url                                    =
"https://jsonplaceholder.typicode.com/pos
ts";

// Initialize cURL session
$ch = curl_init();

// Set cURL options
curl_setopt($ch, CURLOPT_URL, $url);
```

```php
curl_setopt($ch,   CURLOPT_RETURNTRANSFER,
true);

// Execute cURL request and get the
response
$response = curl_exec($ch);

// Check for errors
if ($response === false) {
    echo "cURL Error: " . curl_error($ch);
} else {
    // Decode JSON response
    $data = json_decode($response, true);
    echo "<pre>";
    print_r($data);  // Display the fetched
posts
    echo "</pre>";
}

// Close the cURL session
curl_close($ch);
?>
```

- o **Explanation**:
  - We use cURL to send a **GET** request to the **JSONPlaceholder API**.
  - The response is returned in JSON format, which is decoded using

`json_decode()` to process the data in PHP.

- We print the fetched data using `print_r()` for display.

Summary

By the end of this chapter, you should be able to:

- Understand and implement **RESTful APIs** and interact with them using PHP.
- Use **cURL** to send and receive data from APIs.
- Create your own simple **RESTful API** using PHP.
- Consume third-party APIs and integrate external data into your PHP applications.

Mastering API integration will enable you to build more complex and feature-rich web applications that interact with other services, databases, and external resources.

CHAPTER 17

SECURITY IN PHP

Overview of Web Security Risks (SQL Injection, XSS, CSRF)

Web security is a critical aspect of PHP web application development. Without proper security measures, your website can be vulnerable to attacks that can compromise user data, expose sensitive information, or allow unauthorized access. This chapter covers some of the most common security risks and how to mitigate them in PHP applications.

1. **SQL Injection**:
    - **SQL injection** is one of the most dangerous and common web security vulnerabilities. It occurs when an attacker manipulates SQL queries by injecting malicious SQL code through user input fields. This can lead to unauthorized access to the database, data theft, or even deletion of data.
    - Example: An attacker could input the following into a login form:

    ```vbnet
    ' OR 1=1 --
    ```

This could bypass authentication if not properly validated, allowing the attacker to log in as any user.

2. **Cross-Site Scripting (XSS)**:

   o **XSS** allows attackers to inject malicious scripts into web pages viewed by other users. The scripts are usually written in JavaScript, and they run in the browser of the victim. This can steal session cookies, deface a website, or carry out other malicious actions.

   o Example: An attacker might inject a script into a comment section, which will run whenever someone else views the comment:

   html

   ```
   <script>alert('You     have     been
   hacked!');</script>
   ```

3. **Cross-Site Request Forgery (CSRF)**:

   o **CSRF** attacks trick the user into performing an action they did not intend to. For example, a user may unknowingly perform actions such as changing their password or transferring funds to an attacker's account.

o CSRF exploits the trust a site has in the user's browser, as it may execute requests using the user's session credentials.

Sanitizing User Input and Preventing SQL Injection

One of the most important steps in securing a PHP application is **validating and sanitizing user input**. This ensures that user-provided data does not include any malicious content that can be used to exploit vulnerabilities like SQL injection.

1. **Sanitizing User Input**:
    o **Sanitizing** means cleaning the input to remove unwanted characters or malicious content.
    o You can use functions like `filter_var()` to sanitize input, for example, by removing HTML tags or ensuring that an email address is valid.

    Example: Sanitizing Email Input:

    php

    ```php
    <?php
    $email    =    filter_var($_POST['email'],
    FILTER_SANITIZE_EMAIL);
    if                 (!filter_var($email,
    FILTER_VALIDATE_EMAIL)) {
    ```

```
    echo "Invalid email format!";
} else {
    echo "Valid email: $email";
}
?>
```

2. **Preventing SQL Injection**:
   o **Prepared Statements**: The most effective way to prevent SQL injection is to use **prepared statements** with **parameterized queries**. This ensures that user input is treated as data rather than executable code.

Example: Preventing SQL Injection with Prepared Statements:

php

```php
<?php
$conn      =      new      mysqli('localhost',
'username', 'password', 'database');

if ($conn->connect_error) {
    die("Connection failed: "  .  $conn-
>connect_error);
}

$email = $_POST['email'];
$password = $_POST['password'];
```

206

```php
// Prepared statement to prevent SQL
injection
$stmt = $conn->prepare("SELECT * FROM users
WHERE email = ? AND password = ?");
$stmt->bind_param("ss",          $email,
$password);   // "ss" means two string
parameters
$stmt->execute();
$result = $stmt->get_result();

if ($result->num_rows > 0) {
    echo "User authenticated.";
} else {
    echo "Invalid credentials.";
}

$stmt->close();
$conn->close();
?>
```

- o **Explanation**:
  - `$stmt->prepare()` prepares a SQL query with placeholders (`?`).
  - `$stmt->bind_param()` binds the actual values to the placeholders.
  - This approach ensures that user input is handled safely and prevents SQL injection attacks.

207

3. **Avoiding Direct SQL Queries**:
   - o Always avoid directly embedding user input in SQL queries. Use prepared statements or an ORM (Object Relational Mapper) like **Doctrine** or **Eloquent** in Laravel to safely interact with databases.

Securing Cookies and Sessions

Sessions and cookies are essential for tracking user state and managing authentication. However, they can also be exploited if not properly secured.

1. **Securing Session Cookies**:
   - o To ensure the security of session cookies, you should configure them with the `Secure`, `HttpOnly`, and `SameSite` attributes.
     - **Secure**: Ensures cookies are only sent over HTTPS.
     - **HttpOnly**: Prevents JavaScript from accessing session cookies, which helps prevent XSS attacks.
     - **SameSite**: Prevents cross-site request forgery (CSRF) by ensuring cookies are only sent in requests originating from the same site.

208

Example: Setting Secure Session Cookies:

```php
php


<?php
session_set_cookie_params([
    'lifetime' => 3600,  // Cookie expires
in 1 hour
    'secure' => true,    // Only sent over
HTTPS
    'httponly' => true,  // Not accessible
via JavaScript
    'samesite' => 'Strict'  // Prevent CSRF
attacks
]);
session_start();
?>
```

2. **Session Security Best Practices**:

   o **Regenerate Session ID**: To prevent session fixation attacks, regenerate the session ID after user authentication.

   Example:

   ```php
   php


   <?php
   session_start();
   ```

209

```
session_regenerate_id(true);        //
Regenerate  session  ID  to  prevent
session fixation
?>
```

o **Session Timeout**: Automatically log out users after a period of inactivity. This can be implemented by storing the last activity time in the session and comparing it against the current time.

Example:

php

```php
<?php
session_start();

// Set session timeout (15 minutes)
$timeout_duration = 900;

if
(isset($_SESSION['last_activity'])
&&              (time()            -
$_SESSION['last_activity'])        >
$timeout_duration) {
    // Session has expired, destroy
it
    session_unset();
```

210

```
session_destroy();
echo "Session expired due to
inactivity.";
} else {
$_SESSION['last_activity']     =
time();  // Update last activity time
}
?>
```

Password Hashing and Authentication

Storing passwords securely is one of the most important aspects of web application security. **Never store plain-text passwords**. Instead, use secure hashing algorithms to store passwords safely.

1. **Password Hashing**:
    o   Use the `password_hash()` function to securely hash passwords before storing them in the database.
    o   Use `password_verify()` to check if the entered password matches the stored hash.

Example: Hashing Passwords:

php

```php
<?php
```

211

```php
// Hash the password before storing it in
the database
$password = 'user_password';
$hashedPassword = password_hash($password,
PASSWORD_DEFAULT);    // PASSWORD_DEFAULT
uses bcrypt
echo $hashedPassword;  // Store this hash
in the database
?>
```

2. **Verifying Passwords**:

   o When a user logs in, you need to verify the password by comparing it to the stored hash in the database using `password_verify()`.

   Example: Verifying Password:

   php

```php
<?php
// Assume we retrieved the hashed password
from the database
$storedHash                          =
'$2y$10$eEJn717V0SOAf8g.bBBp9y.Jz6ryOiCkk
BOFvYe40f.IpZRR5y5uS';  // Example hash

$inputPassword = 'user_password';  // The
password entered by the user
```

```
if        (password_verify($inputPassword,
$storedHash)) {
    echo "Password is correct!";
} else {
    echo "Invalid password!";
}
?>
```

- o **Explanation**:
  - password_hash() generates a secure hash of the password, which is then stored in the database.
  - password_verify() checks if the user-entered password matches the stored hash.

3. **Using Salt**:
   - o In modern hashing algorithms like bcrypt, the salt is automatically generated and stored as part of the hash. This makes it more secure than older methods, such as MD5 or SHA1, which are vulnerable to rainbow table attacks.

213

Summary

By the end of this chapter, you should be able to:

- Understand and mitigate common web security risks such as **SQL injection**, **XSS**, and **CSRF**.
- **Sanitize user input** and use **prepared statements** to prevent SQL injection attacks.
- **Secure cookies and sessions** to protect against unauthorized access and ensure session integrity.
- Use **password hashing** techniques to securely store and verify user passwords.

Security is a critical aspect of any web application, and following best practices like those outlined in this chapter will help protect your application from common vulnerabilities and attacks.

CHAPTER 18

PHP AND AJAX: ASYNCHRONOUS WEB DEVELOPMENT

Introduction to AJAX (Asynchronous JavaScript and XML)

AJAX (Asynchronous JavaScript and XML) is a technique used in web development to create dynamic and interactive web applications. With AJAX, web pages can update parts of their content without needing to reload the entire page. This provides a smoother, more responsive user experience by enabling asynchronous communication between the client (browser) and the server.

1. **What is AJAX?**:
    - o **Asynchronous**: AJAX allows the client to send requests to the server and receive responses asynchronously without blocking the page or requiring a full page reload. This results in faster, more dynamic web pages.
    - o **JavaScript**: JavaScript is used to send and receive data to and from the server without refreshing the entire page.

- o **XML**: While AJAX originally used XML to exchange data, today it commonly uses **JSON** because it's lighter and easier to work with in JavaScript.

2. **How AJAX Works**:
   - o **Request**: JavaScript (typically using the `XMLHttpRequest` object or `fetch()` API) sends an asynchronous request to the server.
   - o **Processing**: The server processes the request and sends back the response (e.g., data or HTML).
   - o **Response**: The client processes the server response and updates only the relevant part of the page without reloading the whole page.

Basic AJAX Flow:

4. The user triggers an action (e.g., button click).
5. JavaScript sends an asynchronous request to the server using `AJAX`.
6. The server processes the request and sends data back (usually in **JSON** or **XML** format).
7. JavaScript processes the response and updates the page accordingly.

216

Using PHP with AJAX for Dynamic Content Updates

PHP can work seamlessly with AJAX to provide dynamic content updates. Instead of reloading the entire page, AJAX allows PHP to fetch data or perform operations on the server and send the result back to the client.

1. **Basic Example of Using PHP with AJAX**: In this example, we'll create a simple application that fetches the current date and time from the server using PHP and AJAX.

   HTML and JavaScript (AJAX):

   html

```html
<!DOCTYPE html>
<html lang="en">
<head>
    <meta charset="UTF-8">
    <title>AJAX with PHP Example</title>
    <script>
        function fetchDateTime() {
            var xhr = new XMLHttpRequest();
            xhr.open("GET", "datetime.php", true);  // Request datetime.php
```

217

```
        xhr.onreadystatechange        =
function() {
            if (xhr.readyState === 4
&& xhr.status === 200) {

document.getElementById("datetime").inner
HTML = xhr.responseText;
                }
            };
            xhr.send();
        }
    </script>
</head>
<body>
    <h1>Current Date and Time</h1>
    <button  onclick="fetchDateTime()">Get
Date and Time</button>
    <p id="datetime"></p>
</body>
</html>
```

PHP (datetime.php):

```php
<?php
echo "The current date and time is: " .
date("Y-m-d H:i:s");
?>
```

- o **Explanation**:
  - The `fetchDateTime()` function is called when the user clicks the button.
  - It makes an AJAX request to `datetime.php` using `XMLHttpRequest`.
  - The server processes the request and sends back the current date and time as a response.
  - The JavaScript updates the `<p>` element with the ID `datetime` with the response from the server.

2. **AJAX with POST Method**: Sometimes, you need to send data to the server, such as user input. In this case, you can use the **POST** method to send the data.

HTML and JavaScript (AJAX with POST):

```html
html

<form id="userForm">
    <label    for="username">Enter    your
name:</label>
    <input    type="text"    id="username"
name="username">
    <button                  type="button"
onclick="submitForm()">Submit</button>
</form>
```

219

```
<div id="response"></div>

<script>
    function submitForm() {
        var              username        =
document.getElementById('username').value
;

        var xhr = new XMLHttpRequest();
        xhr.open("POST",        "submit.php",
true);

        xhr.setRequestHeader("Content-
type",             "application/x-www-form-
urlencoded");

        xhr.onreadystatechange          =
function() {
            if (xhr.readyState === 4 &&
xhr.status === 200) {

document.getElementById("response").inner
HTML = xhr.responseText;
            }
        };

        xhr.send("username="              +
encodeURIComponent(username));
    }
</script>
```

PHP (submit.php):

```
php
```

```php
<?php
if (isset($_POST['username'])) {
    $username                           =
htmlspecialchars($_POST['username']);
    echo "Hello, $username!";
} else {
    echo "No name provided!";
}
?>
```

- o **Explanation**:
  - When the user enters their name and clicks the "Submit" button, the submitForm() function is triggered.
  - It sends the entered username to submit.php using the **POST** method.
  - PHP processes the data and sends back a personalized greeting, which is displayed on the page.

Handling Asynchronous Requests in PHP

When handling asynchronous requests in PHP, it's important to understand that the server-side PHP script may be invoked in a non-blocking manner, meaning the server doesn't wait for the request to complete before sending the response.

221

1. **Handling Asynchronous Requests Efficiently**:
    - o Since AJAX requests are asynchronous, you should ensure that the PHP script is optimized for handling multiple requests simultaneously. This can include proper session handling, ensuring that the server responds quickly, and using techniques like **caching** to improve performance.

2. **Asynchronous Request Handling Example**: Here's an example of using AJAX to fetch posts from a database asynchronously. The data is returned as JSON, and the client-side JavaScript updates the HTML dynamically.

HTML and JavaScript (AJAX with JSON):

html

```
<button          onclick="loadPosts()">Load
Posts</button>
<ul id="postList"></ul>

<script>
    function loadPosts() {
        var xhr = new XMLHttpRequest();
        xhr.open("GET", "fetch_posts.php",
true);
        xhr.onreadystatechange          =
function() {
```

```
            if (xhr.readyState === 4 &&
xhr.status === 200) {
                var        posts        =
JSON.parse(xhr.responseText);
                var        list         =
document.getElementById('postList');
                list.innerHTML = '';

posts.forEach(function(post) {
                    var        li        =
document.createElement('li');
                    li.textContent        =
post.title;
                    list.appendChild(li);
                });
            }
        };
        xhr.send();
    }
</script>
```

PHP (fetch_posts.php):

```
php
```

```php
<?php
// Simulating fetching posts from a
database
$posts = [
    ['title' => 'Post 1'],
```

223

```
        ['title' => 'Post 2'],
        ['title' => 'Post 3']
];


// Return posts as JSON
echo json_encode($posts);
?>
```

- o **Explanation**:
  - The `loadPosts()` function makes an AJAX request to `fetch_posts.php`.
  - The server returns the posts as a JSON object, and JavaScript dynamically updates the HTML with the retrieved posts.

---

jQuery and AJAX in PHP Applications

jQuery is a JavaScript library that simplifies working with AJAX requests. It provides an easier way to handle asynchronous requests compared to vanilla JavaScript. jQuery also makes it easier to manipulate the DOM and handle events.

1. **Using jQuery to Send AJAX Requests**: jQuery's `$.ajax()` method makes it easier to send asynchronous requests and handle responses.

Example: Using jQuery to Fetch Posts:

html

```
<button id="loadPosts">Load Posts</button>
<ul id="postList"></ul>

<script
src="https://code.jquery.com/jquery-
3.6.0.min.js"></script>
<script>
    $('#loadPosts').click(function() {
        $.ajax({
            url: 'fetch_posts.php',
            type: 'GET',
            dataType: 'json',
            success: function(posts) {
                var list = $('#postList');
                list.empty();

posts.forEach(function(post) {
                    list.append('<li>'    +
post.title + '</li>');
                });
            }
        });
    });
</script>
```

PHP (fetch_posts.php):

225

php

```php
<?php
// Simulating fetching posts from a
database
$posts = [
    ['title' => 'Post 1'],
    ['title' => 'Post 2'],
    ['title' => 'Post 3']
];

// Return posts as JSON
echo json_encode($posts);
?>
```

- o **Explanation**:
    - jQuery's `$.ajax()` method sends a **GET** request to `fetch_posts.php`.
    - When the response is received (in JSON format), the success callback updates the HTML by appending each post to the list.

2. **Advantages of Using jQuery**:
    - o **Simplicity**: jQuery simplifies AJAX syntax, making it easier to work with.
    - o **Cross-Browser Compatibility**: jQuery handles differences between browsers, ensuring the code works consistently across platforms.

226

o **Enhanced Features**: jQuery provides additional utilities like animation and DOM manipulation, which can enhance the user experience.

Summary

By the end of this chapter, you should be able to:

- Understand the basic concepts of **AJAX** and how it works with PHP to create dynamic and interactive web applications.
- Use **PHP** with **AJAX** to fetch and send data asynchronously, allowing for real-time updates on the page.
- Handle asynchronous requests in PHP and **JSON** for efficient data exchange.
- Use **jQuery** to simplify the process of making AJAX requests and updating the DOM dynamically.

AJAX, when combined with PHP, enables the development of fast, interactive web applications that offer a more seamless user experience by reducing the need for page reloads.

CHAPTER 19

WORKING WITH FRAMEWORKS IN PHP

Introduction to PHP Frameworks (Laravel, Symfony, CodeIgniter)

PHP frameworks are pre-built collections of libraries and tools that simplify and streamline the development of web applications. These frameworks follow the **MVC (Model-View-Controller)** architectural pattern and provide reusable components, helping developers write clean, maintainable, and secure code. There are several popular PHP frameworks, each with its strengths and trade-offs. In this chapter, we'll discuss three widely-used PHP frameworks: **Laravel**, **Symfony**, and **CodeIgniter**.

1. **Laravel**:
   - **Laravel** is one of the most popular and modern PHP frameworks. It is known for its elegant syntax and features that enhance productivity. It includes tools for routing, database migrations, authentication, testing, and more.
   - Laravel uses **Eloquent ORM** for database interactions and provides a built-in templating engine called **Blade** for views.

228

- o Laravel is great for large-scale applications and has a rich ecosystem with packages like **Laravel Forge** (for server management), **Laravel Passport** (for API authentication), and **Laravel Horizon** (for queue monitoring).

Key Features of Laravel:

- o **Eloquent ORM** for database management.
- o **Blade templating engine** for views.
- o **Built-in authentication and authorization**.
- o **Artisan CLI** for task automation.
- o **Routing, middleware, and controllers** for web and API development.

2. **Symfony**:

- o **Symfony** is a highly flexible and robust PHP framework, known for its reusability of components. It is widely used in enterprise-level applications.
- o Symfony is often chosen for **large-scale applications** due to its flexibility and use of components that can be used independently in other projects.
- o Symfony provides **Twig** for templating, and it supports **Doctrine ORM** for database interactions.

Key Features of Symfony:

- o **Reusable components** for building modular applications.
- o **Twig templating engine**.
- o **Doctrine ORM** for database abstraction.
- o **Highly customizable** and suited for enterprise solutions.

3. **CodeIgniter**:

- o **CodeIgniter** is a lightweight PHP framework that is simple to set up and use, making it ideal for small to medium-sized projects. It's known for its **small footprint** and **fast performance**.
- o CodeIgniter does not impose a strict MVC structure, giving developers flexibility to structure their code in a way that works best for their project.
- o It includes built-in libraries for common tasks like form validation, session management, and database interaction.

Key Features of CodeIgniter:

- o **Small footprint** and fast performance.
- o **Less restrictive** MVC structure, allowing for more flexibility.
- o **Built-in helpers and libraries**.

230

o   Ideal for **small to medium-sized applications**.

Choosing the Right Framework for Your Project

Choosing the right PHP framework depends on your project's requirements, the size of your application, your team's experience, and the features you need. Here are some factors to consider when selecting a PHP framework:

1. **Project Size and Complexity**:
    o   **Laravel** is ideal for **large-scale applications** with complex requirements due to its rich ecosystem and features like authentication, queuing, and real-time notifications.
    o   **Symfony** is suitable for **enterprise-level applications** that require flexibility, modularity, and reusable components.
    o   **CodeIgniter** is great for **small to medium-sized projects** or when you need a framework that's easy to set up and doesn't impose many restrictions.

2. **Community and Ecosystem**:
    o   **Laravel** has a large and active community with tons of tutorials, plugins, and third-party integrations. If you need support, **Laravel's**

      ecosystem (Forge, Envoyer, etc.) can provide a lot of value.

- o **Symfony** has a strong enterprise presence and is widely used in large, complex systems.
- o **CodeIgniter** is also popular but has a smaller community compared to Laravel and Symfony.

3. **Learning Curve**:

- o **Laravel** has a moderate learning curve, especially if you are new to PHP frameworks. However, its excellent documentation and strong community support make it easy to pick up.
- o **Symfony** has a steeper learning curve, especially due to its modular nature. It's great if you need high customizability but can be more challenging for beginners.
- o **CodeIgniter** has a minimal learning curve and is straightforward for developers with basic PHP knowledge.

4. **Performance**:

- o **Laravel** offers great performance but can be more resource-intensive due to its rich set of features.
- o **Symfony** is highly flexible, but performance can be a concern for very lightweight applications.
- o **CodeIgniter** is lightweight and fast, making it ideal for projects where speed is crucial.

Setting Up a PHP Framework

In this section, we'll walk through the steps to set up **Laravel**, one of the most popular PHP frameworks, on your local development environment.

1. **Prerequisites**:
   - You need to have **PHP** and **Composer** installed on your system. Composer is a dependency manager for PHP that Laravel uses for managing packages.
   - Ensure that you have a **local web server** (like **XAMPP**, **MAMP**, or **Homestead**) running.

2. **Installing Laravel**: The easiest way to install Laravel is through **Composer**. You can either create a new Laravel project or install Laravel globally on your system.
   - **Install Laravel using Composer**:

   ```bash
   bash


   composer create-project --prefer-
   dist laravel/laravel myapp
   ```

   This command creates a new Laravel project called `myapp`.

3. **Setting Up the Environment**:

233

o   After installing Laravel, navigate to the project directory:

```bash

cd myapp
```

o   Laravel uses **.env** files for environment configuration (database credentials, application key, etc.). You'll need to configure your environment settings in the .env file.

4. **Starting the Development Server**: Laravel comes with a built-in development server that you can use to run your application locally. Run the following command to start the server:

```bash

php artisan serve
```

This command will start the development server and you can access the application at http://localhost:8000.

Basic Routing and Controller Setup in Laravel

One of the key features of Laravel is its powerful routing system. In this section, we'll cover how to define routes and set up controllers in Laravel.

1. **Defining Routes**: Routes in Laravel are defined in the `routes/web.php` file. You can define routes that respond to different HTTP methods (GET, POST, etc.).

   Example: Basic Route in `web.php`:

   ```php
   php

   use Illuminate\Support\Facades\Route;

   Route::get('/', function () {
       return view('welcome');
   });
   ```

   o The above route handles the **GET** request to the homepage (`/`) and returns a view called `welcome`.

2. **Creating a Controller**: Laravel allows you to easily generate controllers using Artisan, the Laravel command-line tool.

   o **Create a Controller**: To create a controller, run the following command:

235

```
bash
```

```
php      artisan      make:controller
PostController
```

- o This will create a new file called PostController.php in the app/Http/Controllers directory.

Example: PostController.php:

```
php
```

```php
<?php

namespace App\Http\Controllers;

use Illuminate\Http\Request;

class PostController extends Controller
{
    public function index()
    {
        return view('posts.index');    // Return the 'index' view for posts
    }

    public function show($id)
    {
```

236

```
      return view('posts.show', ['id' =>
$id]);  // Show post with the given ID
   }
}
```

- o The `PostController` has two methods:
  - **`index()`**: Displays all posts.
  - **`show($id)`**: Displays a single post based on the ID.

3. **Assigning Routes to Controllers**: You can assign routes to controller methods using the `Route::get()` method, or use route groups for more advanced routing.

Example: Assigning Routes to Controller Methods:

php

```
Route::get('/posts',
[PostController::class, 'index']);    //
Route to show all posts
Route::get('/posts/{id}',
[PostController::class, 'show']);    //
Route to show a specific post by ID
```

- o This creates two routes:
  - GET /posts: Maps to the `index()` method of `PostController`.

- GET /posts/{id}: Maps to the show($id) method of PostController, where {id} is a dynamic parameter.

4. **Creating Views**: Views are stored in the resources/views directory. In this example, you would create a posts/index.blade.php file to display the list of posts.

Example: Creating a Blade View:

php

```
<!-- resources/views/posts/index.blade.php
-->
<h1>All Posts</h1>
<ul>
    <li><a href="/posts/1">Post 1</a></li>
    <li><a href="/posts/2">Post 2</a></li>
    <li><a href="/posts/3">Post 3</a></li>
</ul>
```

- o The Blade templating engine allows you to embed PHP in HTML files, and provides an easy syntax for rendering views and handling logic.

238

Summary

By the end of this chapter, you should be able to:

- Understand the basics of **PHP frameworks** like **Laravel**, **Symfony**, and **CodeIgniter**.
- Choose the right framework for your project based on its features, scalability, and community support.
- Set up a **PHP framework** like Laravel, configure the environment, and start the development server.
- Define basic **routes** and **controllers** in Laravel and connect them with views using the **Blade templating engine**.

Working with PHP frameworks like Laravel can significantly speed up development and help you build maintainable, scalable, and secure web applications. In the next chapter, we'll dive deeper into advanced features of Laravel to further enhance your application.

CHAPTER 20

ADVANCED DATABASE TECHNIQUES

Database Normalization and Optimization

Database normalization is the process of organizing a database in such a way that redundancy is minimized, and data integrity is maintained. By dividing large tables into smaller, more manageable pieces and defining relationships between them, normalization reduces the risk of anomalies (like insertion, update, and deletion anomalies).

1. **What is Database Normalization?**
   - o Normalization ensures that each piece of data is stored only once, which helps to eliminate redundancy and inconsistency. It involves creating tables in a way that dependencies are logical and consistent.

2. **Normalization Forms**: There are several levels of normalization, known as **normal forms** (1NF, 2NF, 3NF, etc.). The goal is to achieve at least **3NF (Third Normal Form)**, which addresses most redundancy issues and ensures data integrity.

240

- o **1NF (First Normal Form)**: Each column must contain atomic (indivisible) values, and each record must be unique.
- o **2NF (Second Normal Form)**: Achieved by eliminating partial dependencies; non-key attributes must depend on the entire primary key.
- o **3NF (Third Normal Form)**: Achieved by eliminating transitive dependencies; non-key attributes must be directly dependent on the primary key.

Example of Database Normalization: Suppose you have the following table to store employee and department information:

less

```
Employees Table:
|  EmployeeID  |  Name   |  Department  |  DepartmentLocation  |
|------------|-------|------------|--------------|
|  1         | Alice | HR         | Building A   |
|  2         | Bob   | IT         | Building B   |
|  3         | Carol | HR         | Building A   |
```

241

To normalize this to **3NF**, you would separate the department details into a separate table to eliminate redundancy.

Normalized Tables:

- **Employees Table**:

```pgsql
| EmployeeID | Name  | DepartmentID
|
|------------|-------|--------------
-|
| 1          | Alice | 1           |
| 2          | Bob   | 2           |
| 3          | Carol | 1           |
```

- **Departments Table**:

```less
|  DepartmentID  |  Department  |
DepartmentLocation  |
|--------------|------------|------
--------------|
| 1            | HR         | Building
A          |
| 2            | IT         | Building
B          |
```

242

In this structure, the data is normalized, reducing redundancy (such as repeating department names and locations in each employee record) and ensuring data integrity.

Indexing and Optimizing Queries for Performance

Indexing is a technique used to improve the speed of data retrieval operations on a database. An index is created on one or more columns of a table and allows the database to locate rows faster than without the index.

1. **What is an Index?**
   - An index is a data structure that helps speed up data retrieval operations on a database. When a query is executed, the database uses the index to find the matching rows much faster.
   - Indexes are especially important for large databases with many rows and frequent queries.

2. **Creating an Index**: You can create an index on one or more columns using the CREATE INDEX statement or while defining a table with the PRIMARY KEY or UNIQUE constraints.

Example: Creating an Index:

```sql
sql
```

243

```
CREATE    INDEX    idx_employee_name    ON
employees (name);
```

- o This index will speed up queries that search for employees by name.

3. **Optimizing Queries**: To improve performance, it's important to optimize your SQL queries by following best practices, such as:
   - o **Using proper indexing**: Index frequently queried columns.
   - o ****Avoiding SELECT *****: Instead of selecting all columns, only retrieve the columns you need.
   - o **Using LIMIT**: If you only need a subset of rows, use LIMIT to avoid unnecessary data retrieval.
   - o **Using JOINs efficiently**: When combining multiple tables, ensure that the columns being joined are indexed.

Example: Optimized Query:

```sql
SELECT  name,  department  FROM  employees
WHERE department = 'HR' LIMIT 10;
```

4. **EXPLAIN Command**: The EXPLAIN command helps analyze the execution plan of a query. It shows how

MySQL plans to execute the query, including which indexes are used, how tables are joined, and the order in which operations are performed.

Example: Using EXPLAIN:

sql

```
EXPLAIN SELECT name, department FROM
employees WHERE department = 'HR';
```

Using JOINs, Subqueries, and Stored Procedures in PHP

1. **Using JOINs in SQL**: **JOIN** operations are used to combine rows from two or more tables based on a related column. The most common types of joins are:
    o   **INNER JOIN**: Returns only matching rows from both tables.
    o   **LEFT JOIN (OUTER JOIN)**: Returns all rows from the left table, and matching rows from the right table.
    o   **RIGHT JOIN**: Returns all rows from the right table, and matching rows from the left table.
    o   **FULL OUTER JOIN**: Returns rows when there is a match in one of the tables.

Example: INNER JOIN:

```sql
sql

SELECT                          employees.name,
departments.department
FROM employees
INNER      JOIN      departments        ON
employees.department_id = departments.id;
```

Using JOINs in PHP: You can execute queries with joins in PHP using PDO or MySQLi.

Example: PHP Code with JOIN:

```php
php

<?php
$pdo                    =                   new
PDO('mysql:host=localhost;dbname=myapp',
'root', '');
$stmt = $pdo->query('
    SELECT                      employees.name,
departments.department
    FROM employees
    INNER      JOIN      departments        ON
employees.department_id = departments.id
');

$employees = $stmt->fetchAll();
foreach ($employees as $employee) {
```

```
    echo "Name: " . $employee['name'] . ",
Department: " . $employee['department'] .
"<br>";
}
?>
```

2. **Using Subqueries**: A **subquery** is a query inside another query. Subqueries are useful when you need to retrieve data based on the results of another query.

   Example: Subquery:

   sql

   ```sql
   SELECT name, department FROM employees
   WHERE department_id = (SELECT id FROM
   departments WHERE department = 'HR');
   ```

3. **Stored Procedures**: A **stored procedure** is a set of SQL statements that can be executed repeatedly. It's stored in the database and can be called from PHP to execute complex operations.

   Example: Creating a Stored Procedure:

   sql

   ```sql
   DELIMITER //
   ```

247

```
CREATE                          PROCEDURE
getEmployeesByDepartment(IN      dept_name
VARCHAR(255))
BEGIN
    SELECT   name   FROM   employees   WHERE
department = dept_name;
END //
DELIMITER ;
```

Calling the Stored Procedure in PHP:

```php
php

<?php
$pdo                    =                    new
PDO('mysql:host=localhost;dbname=myapp',
'root', '');
$stmt           =           $pdo->prepare("CALL
getEmployeesByDepartment(:dept_name)");
$stmt->bindParam(':dept_name',
$departmentName);
$departmentName = 'HR';
$stmt->execute();

$employees = $stmt->fetchAll();
foreach ($employees as $employee) {
    echo "Name: " . $employee['name'] .
"<br>";
}
?>
```

Managing Relationships (One-to-Many, Many-to-Many)

Managing relationships between tables is a key aspect of database design. Relationships describe how different entities (tables) in the database are connected to each other.

1. **One-to-Many Relationship**: A one-to-many relationship means that one record in the parent table can be related to many records in the child table.

   Example: One-to-Many (One department has many employees):

   o **Departments Table**: Stores department details.
   o **Employees Table**: Stores employee details, each employee belongs to one department.

   SQL Example:

   sql

```
SELECT                    employees.name,
departments.department
FROM employees
INNER      JOIN     departments      ON
employees.department_id = departments.id;
```

2. **Many-to-Many Relationship**: A many-to-many relationship means that one record in the first table can be

related to many records in the second table, and vice versa. This is usually managed through a **junction table** (also called a **bridge table**).

Example: Many-to-Many (A student can enroll in many courses, and each course can have many students):

- o **Students Table**: Stores student information.
- o **Courses Table**: Stores course information.
- o **Student_Course Table**: Junction table to link students and courses.

SQL Example:

sql

```
SELECT students.name, courses.course_name
FROM students
INNER JOIN student_course ON students.id =
student_course.student_id
INNER      JOIN      courses      ON
student_course.course_id = courses.id;
```

3. **Using Foreign Keys**: In relational databases, foreign keys are used to establish and enforce a link between the data in two tables, ensuring referential integrity.

Example: Creating Foreign Key Relationship:

```sql
sql

CREATE TABLE employees (
    id INT AUTO_INCREMENT PRIMARY KEY,
    name VARCHAR(100),
    department_id INT,
    FOREIGN KEY (department_id) REFERENCES
departments(id)
);
```

Summary

By the end of this chapter, you should be able to:

- **Normalize** databases and understand how to design them to reduce redundancy and maintain integrity.
- Use **indexes** to optimize database queries for better performance.
- Leverage **JOINs**, **subqueries**, and **stored procedures** to retrieve and manipulate data efficiently in PHP applications.
- Understand and manage **one-to-many** and **many-to-many** relationships between database tables.

Mastering these advanced database techniques will significantly improve the performance, scalability, and maintainability of your PHP applications. In the next chapter, you will learn how to integrate these techniques with PHP frameworks to build robust applications.

CHAPTER 21

TESTING AND DEBUGGING PHP APPLICATIONS

Writing and Running Unit Tests in PHP

Unit testing is a method of testing individual units of code (usually functions or methods) in isolation. The goal is to ensure that each unit of the application behaves as expected. In PHP, unit tests can be written using various testing frameworks, with **PHPUnit** being one of the most popular.

1. **What is a Unit Test?**
    - o A **unit test** is a small, automated test that checks the functionality of a specific part of the codebase, such as a method or function. These tests are typically isolated from the rest of the application to ensure that the tested unit behaves as expected without dependencies or side effects.
2. **Setting Up PHPUnit**: PHPUnit is the most widely used testing framework for PHP. You can install PHPUnit using **Composer**.
    - o **Installing PHPUnit**: To install PHPUnit globally using Composer:

```bash
```

253

```
composer          require          --dev
phpunit/phpunit
```

o **Basic PHPUnit Test**: To create a basic unit test, you need to write a test class that extends `PHPUnit\Framework\TestCase`. Each test method should start with the `test` prefix and will typically assert that a function returns the expected result.

Example: Basic PHPUnit Test:

```php
php
```

```php
<?php
use PHPUnit\Framework\TestCase;

class CalculatorTest extends TestCase {
    public function testAdd() {
        $calculator = new Calculator();
        $this->assertEquals(5,
$calculator->add(2, 3));   // Asserts that
2 + 3 equals 5
    }

    public function testSubtract() {
        $calculator = new Calculator();
```

254

```
        $this->assertEquals(1,
$calculator->subtract(3, 2));   // Asserts
that 3 - 2 equals 1
    }
}
```

- o **Explanation**:
  - `testAdd()` and `testSubtract()` are test methods. They create a `Calculator` object and assert that the `add()` and `subtract()` methods work as expected.
  - `assertEquals()` checks if the expected result matches the actual result.

3. **Running PHPUnit Tests**: Once you have written your test cases, you can run them from the command line using the following command:

```bash

```

```
./vendor/bin/phpunit
tests/CalculatorTest.php
```

PHPUnit will execute the tests and display the results in the terminal.

Debugging Techniques (Using Xdebug)

Xdebug is a powerful tool that helps you debug PHP applications by providing a step-by-step walkthrough of your code, inspecting variables, and analyzing execution flow. Xdebug integrates with popular IDEs like PhpStorm and Visual Studio Code to provide advanced debugging features.

1. **Installing Xdebug**: Xdebug can be installed via **PECL** or directly through package managers like `apt` or `brew`. For example, to install Xdebug using PECL, run:

   bash

   ```
   pecl install xdebug
   ```

2. **Configuring Xdebug**: After installing Xdebug, you need to configure it by editing your `php.ini` file. Here's an example configuration for Xdebug:

   ini

   ```
   [xdebug]
   zend_extension="/path/to/xdebug.so"
   xdebug.mode=debug
   xdebug.start_with_request=yes
   xdebug.client_host=127.0.0.1
   xdebug.client_port=9003
   ```

- o **Explanation**:
  - `zend_extension`: Specifies the path to the Xdebug extension.
  - `xdebug.mode`: Sets the mode for Xdebug. `debug` mode enables remote debugging.
  - `xdebug.start_with_request`: Ensures that Xdebug starts automatically when you run a request.
  - `xdebug.client_host`: Specifies the IP address of your IDE or debugger.
  - `xdebug.client_port`: Specifies the port number (default is 9003).

3. **Using Xdebug**:
   - o Once Xdebug is installed and configured, you can start debugging by setting breakpoints in your code (using your IDE).
   - o When the PHP script reaches a breakpoint, the execution pauses, allowing you to inspect variables, step through the code, and evaluate expressions in real-time.

Example: Step-by-Step Debugging:

- o Set a breakpoint in your code at the line where you want the debugger to pause (e.g., in `Calculator.php`).

257

- o Run your PHP script from the command line or via the browser.
- o Xdebug will pause execution at the breakpoint, allowing you to inspect the call stack, variables, and other details.

Error Logging and Handling in PHP

Error logging and handling in PHP are critical to ensuring that your application runs smoothly and that issues are identified and addressed quickly.

1. **PHP Error Reporting**: PHP provides several built-in functions for controlling error reporting and logging. The `error_reporting()` function sets which types of errors are reported, and the `ini_set()` function can be used to configure logging behavior.

   Example: Enabling Error Reporting:

   php

   ```php
   <?php
   error_reporting(E_ALL);    // Report all
   errors, warnings, and notices
   ini_set('display_errors', 1);  // Display
   errors in the browser
   ```

- o **Explanation**:
  - ▪ E_ALL reports all types of errors.
  - ▪ display_errors enables error display in the browser (useful during development but should be disabled in production).

2. **Logging Errors to a File**: You can log errors to a file by setting log_errors and specifying a log file in the php.ini file or dynamically using ini_set().

Example: Logging Errors to a File:

php

```php
<?php
ini_set('log_errors', 1);
ini_set('error_log',        '/path/to/php-
error.log');
```

- o This configuration logs errors to the specified file (/path/to/php-error.log).

3. **Custom Error Handling**: PHP allows you to create custom error handlers using the set_error_handler() function. This is useful if you want to define how errors are handled (e.g., logging errors, displaying custom error messages).

Example: Custom Error Handler:

php

```php
<?php
function        customErrorHandler($errno,
$errstr, $errfile, $errline) {
    echo  "Error  [$errno]:  $errstr  in
$errfile on line $errline\n";
}

set_error_handler("customErrorHandler");

// Trigger an error
echo $undefinedVar;   // Notice: Undefined
variable
?>
```

- o **Explanation**:
  - The `customErrorHandler()` function is called whenever an error occurs.
  - It takes parameters such as the error number, message, file, and line number.

4. **Exception Handling**: **Exceptions** provide a more robust way of handling errors in PHP. They allow you to catch and manage errors that occur in your application.

Example: Using try-catch Blocks:

php

```php
<?php
try {
    $num = 10;
    if ($num < 20) {
        throw new Exception("Number is too small.");
    }
} catch (Exception $e) {
    echo 'Caught exception: ', $e->getMessage();
}
?>
```

- o **Explanation**:
    - In this example, if `$num` is less than 20, an exception is thrown with the message `"Number is too small."`.
    - The `catch` block handles the exception and displays the error message.

Using PHPUnit for Test-Driven Development (TDD)

Test-Driven Development (TDD) is a software development methodology where tests are written before writing the actual code. PHPUnit is a testing framework that enables developers to practice TDD in PHP.

261

1. **What is TDD?**:

    o TDD follows a simple cycle: **Red, Green, Refactor**.

        1. **Red**: Write a test that fails because the feature has not been implemented yet.

        2. **Green**: Write just enough code to pass the test.

        3. **Refactor**: Clean up the code while keeping the tests passing.

2. **Creating Tests with PHPUnit**: With PHPUnit, you can write tests that describe how your application should behave. Tests are typically written in the form of assertions that verify expected outcomes.

    Example: Writing Tests in TDD:

    o Let's assume you are building a `Calculator` class. The first step in TDD is to write a test for the `add` method.

    Step 1: Write the Test:

    php

```php
<?php
use PHPUnit\Framework\TestCase;

class CalculatorTest extends TestCase {
```

```php
public function testAdd() {
    $calculator = new Calculator();
    $this->assertEquals(5,
$calculator->add(2, 3));  // Test that 2 +
3 equals 5
    }
}
```

Step 2: Write the Code to Pass the Test:

php

```php
<?php
class Calculator {
    public function add($a, $b) {
        return $a + $b;      // Simple
implementation
    }
}
```

Step 3: Refactor:

o   Once the test passes, you can refactor the code to improve performance or readability while ensuring that all tests still pass.

3. **Running PHPUnit Tests**: After writing the tests, you can run them using the PHPUnit command-line tool.

bash

```
./vendor/bin/phpunit
tests/CalculatorTest.php
```

PHPUnit will execute the tests and display whether they passed or failed.

Summary

By the end of this chapter, you should be able to:

- Write and run **unit tests** using **PHPUnit** to ensure your PHP code behaves as expected.
- Use **Xdebug** for **debugging PHP applications** with breakpoints and detailed stack traces.
- Configure **error logging** and **custom error handling** in PHP to manage and log errors effectively.
- Implement **test-driven development (TDD)** with PHPUnit, following the **Red-Green-Refactor** cycle.

Testing and debugging are crucial steps in the development process that help ensure your application works correctly and is easy to maintain. By incorporating TDD and using tools like PHPUnit and Xdebug, you can build robust, reliable, and efficient PHP applications.

CHAPTER 22

DEPLOYING PHP APPLICATIONS

Preparing Your PHP Application for Deployment

Deploying a PHP application involves moving it from a development environment (usually on your local machine) to a live production server. This process requires careful preparation to ensure your application is secure, optimized, and scalable.

1. **Code Optimization**:
   - o **Remove Unnecessary Files**: Before deploying your application, ensure that development-related files (like test scripts, debug files, or unused libraries) are removed from the production environment.
   - o **Minify CSS and JavaScript**: Minifying your CSS and JavaScript files reduces file size and speeds up page loading time by eliminating unnecessary spaces and characters.
   - o **Optimize Database Queries**: Ensure that queries are optimized to handle larger datasets efficiently in a production environment. Use proper indexes, avoid `SELECT *` queries, and ensure that queries are fast and efficient.

2. **Configuration Settings**:

265

- o **Environment Variables**: Use environment-specific configuration files (.env) to store sensitive information such as database credentials, API keys, and other secrets. This allows you to easily switch between development, staging, and production environments without modifying the codebase.

- o **Error Reporting**: Ensure that error reporting is disabled in the production environment to prevent sensitive information from being exposed to users. Use `ini_set('display_errors', 0)` and log errors to a file instead.

```php
ini_set('display_errors', 0);
ini_set('log_errors', 1);
ini_set('error_log',
'/path/to/error_log');
```

3. **Database Migration**:

- o Before deploying your application, ensure that the production database schema is up-to-date. You can use **database migration tools** like Laravel's migrations or Symfony's Doctrine migrations to version and automate changes to the database schema.

- o Ensure that any new database tables, columns, or indexes are added in the production environment.

4. **Security Considerations**:

   - o **Input Validation and Sanitization**: Ensure all user inputs are validated and sanitized to prevent **SQL injection**, **XSS**, and other types of attacks.

   - o **HTTPS**: Ensure your website is using **SSL** (Secure Socket Layer) to encrypt traffic between the client and server. You can use **Let's Encrypt** for a free SSL certificate or purchase one from a certificate authority.

Using FTP/SFTP for File Transfer

Once your PHP application is ready for deployment, you'll need to transfer your files from your local environment to your web server. You can do this using **FTP (File Transfer Protocol)** or **SFTP (Secure File Transfer Protocol)**.

1. **FTP vs SFTP**:

   - o **FTP** is an insecure protocol that sends data in plaintext, including your login credentials.

   - o **SFTP** is a more secure version of FTP. It encrypts the connection, protecting your data during transfer.

2. **Using FTP/SFTP for File Transfer**:

- o You can use FTP/SFTP clients like **FileZilla** or **WinSCP** to upload your PHP files to the server. You'll need the server's hostname, your FTP/SFTP username, and password to authenticate.

3. **File Transfer Process**:

   - o **Connect to the Server**: Open your FTP/SFTP client and enter the credentials provided by your hosting provider.

   - o **Upload Files**: Navigate to the directory on your local machine where your PHP files are stored, and upload them to the appropriate directory on the server (usually the `public_html` or `www` folder).

   - o **Set File Permissions**: After uploading, set appropriate permissions for the files and directories on the server. For example:

     - Files: `644` (readable by everyone, writable by owner)

     - Directories: `755` (readable, writable, and executable by owner)

   - o Ensure that sensitive files (like `.env` files) are properly secured and not accessible via the web server.

Setting Up a Production Environment (Web Server, Databases, and Security)

To host your PHP application in production, you'll need a properly configured production environment. This includes setting up a **web server**, **database**, and ensuring **security**.

1. **Web Server Setup**: The most commonly used web servers for PHP are **Apache** and **Nginx**. You'll need to configure the web server to serve PHP files.

   o **Apache**:
      ▪ Install Apache on your server:

      bash

      ```
      sudo apt-get install apache2
      ```

      ▪ Ensure that Apache is configured to handle PHP requests by enabling the PHP module:

      bash

      ```
      sudo       apt-get       install
      libapache2-mod-php
      sudo systemctl restart apache2
      ```

   o **Nginx**:
      ▪ Install Nginx:

269

```bash
bash

sudo apt-get install nginx
```

- Configure Nginx to work with PHP by setting up a PHP-FPM (FastCGI Process Manager) configuration.
- Example configuration (`/etc/nginx/sites-available/default`):

```nginx
nginx

server {
    listen 80;
    server_name example.com;
    root /var/www/html;

    index index.php;

    location ~ \.php$ {
        fastcgi_pass
unix:/var/run/php/php7.4-
fpm.sock;
        fastcgi_index
index.php;
        include
fastcgi_params;
    }
```

270

}

2. **Database Setup**:

   o Install a database system such as **MySQL** or **PostgreSQL**. For MySQL, run the following:

   bash

   ```
   sudo apt-get install mysql-server
   sudo systemctl start mysql
   ```

   o Configure the database to accept remote connections if necessary. Ensure that the user and permissions are set correctly to interact with the database.

   o Import your database schema into the production environment using tools like **phpMyAdmin**, **MySQL Workbench**, or command-line tools.

3. **Security Setup**:

   o **SSL (HTTPS)**: Set up SSL to encrypt communication between the client and the server. You can use **Let's Encrypt** for a free SSL certificate or buy one from a certificate authority.

   bash

   ```
   sudo   apt-get   install   certbot
   python3-certbot-nginx
   ```

271

```
sudo certbot --nginx
```

o **Firewall**: Configure your server's firewall to allow only necessary ports (e.g., HTTP/HTTPS, SSH) and block unnecessary ports.

o **Permissions**: Ensure that the correct file permissions are set for your web server's root directory. For example, avoid giving write permissions to files that should only be readable.

o **Keep Software Up-to-Date**: Regularly update your PHP version, web server, and any third-party libraries or frameworks you use.

Continuous Deployment and Version Control (Git)

Continuous deployment (CD) is the practice of automatically deploying code to production after it passes all tests and builds. **Version control** (using **Git**) helps you track changes, collaborate with team members, and manage deployment versions.

1. **Version Control with Git**:

   o Git is a powerful version control system that allows you to track changes in your codebase over time. It helps developers work collaboratively and manage different versions of an application.

272

o **Initializing a Git Repository**:

```bash
git init
```

- This initializes a new Git repository in your project directory.

o **Committing Changes**:

```bash
git add .
git commit -m "Initial commit"
```

o **Pushing Code to a Remote Repository**: To push your code to a remote repository (e.g., GitHub, GitLab), first, create a remote repository and then add it:

```bash
git remote add origin https://github.com/yourusername/repository.git
git push -u origin master
```

2. **Continuous Deployment (CD)**:

- o **Using CI/CD Tools**: Tools like **Jenkins, GitLab CI**, and **GitHub Actions** help automate the deployment process. These tools can be configured to deploy code automatically to your production server after passing tests.

- o **Example: Using GitHub Actions for CD**: GitHub Actions allows you to automate workflows. You can create a `.github/workflows/deploy.yml` file to define the steps for continuous deployment, such as:

  - Checking out the code from GitHub.
  - Installing dependencies.
  - Running tests.
  - Deploying to a server via SSH or FTP.

```yaml
name: Deploy to Server

on:
  push:
    branches:
      - master

jobs:
  deploy:
    runs-on: ubuntu-latest
```

```
steps:
  - name: Checkout code
    uses: actions/checkout@v2

  - name: Deploy to server
    run: |
      ssh                 -i              ${{
secrets.SSH_PRIVATE_KEY                   }}
username@server.com "cd /var/www/html &&
git pull origin master && composer install"
```

3. **Automated Deployment**:

   o   Automate your deployments using tools like
       Envoyer (for Laravel) or **Deployer** for PHP.
       These tools help automate the entire process,
       from pulling the latest changes to your server to
       clearing caches.

Summary

By the end of this chapter, you should be able to:

- Prepare your **PHP application** for deployment by
  optimizing code and configuring environment settings.
- Use **FTP/SFTP** to transfer files to the production server
  securely.

275

- Set up a **production environment** including web server configuration (Apache, Nginx), database setup, and security measures (SSL, firewall).
- Implement **continuous deployment** using version control (Git) and tools like **GitHub Actions**, **Jenkins**, or **GitLab CI**.

By following best practices for deployment, version control, and continuous integration, you can ensure that your PHP application is stable, secure, and easy to maintain in a production environment.

CHAPTER 23

PERFORMANCE OPTIMIZATION FOR PHP WEB APPLICATIONS

Profiling PHP Applications and Finding Bottlenecks

Profiling is the process of measuring the performance of a PHP application to identify parts of the code that are slowing down execution. Profiling tools help developers pinpoint performance bottlenecks, which can be optimized for faster and more efficient applications.

1. **What is Profiling?**: Profiling involves tracking the performance of your PHP code and identifying functions or operations that take up the most time and resources. Profiling can reveal problems such as inefficient loops, excessive database queries, or slow third-party API calls.

2. **Using Xdebug for Profiling**: **Xdebug** is a PHP extension that provides powerful debugging and profiling capabilities. It can generate **execution traces** and **profiling data** that help you identify performance bottlenecks.

   o **Installing Xdebug**: Install Xdebug via **PECL**:

   bash

```
pecl install xdebug
```

o **Enabling Profiling in Xdebug**: In your `php.ini` file, enable profiling:

```
ini
```

```
[xdebug]
zend_extension="xdebug.so"
xdebug.profiler_enable=1
xdebug.profiler_output_dir="/path/t
o/profiler_output"
```

o **Generating Profiling Data**: Xdebug will generate profiling files in the specified output directory. These files are typically saved with a `.cachegrind` extension, which can be analyzed using **KCachegrind** or **Webgrind** (a web-based Xdebug profiler).

o **Analyzing Profiling Data**: You can use tools like **KCachegrind** or **Webgrind** to open the `.cachegrind` file and analyze the profiling results. These tools visualize the call graph and show which functions consume the most time.

3. **Profiling with Blackfire**: **Blackfire** is another powerful profiling tool that is integrated with PHP. It offers both code profiling and performance benchmarking for PHP applications.

How to Use Blackfire:

- o Install Blackfire on your system and integrate it into your application.
- o Run performance profiling with a simple command:

```bash

blackfire run php your-application.php
```

Analysis: Blackfire provides detailed insights into function calls, their execution time, and memory consumption, making it easier to identify and optimize performance bottlenecks.

Caching Strategies (File Caching, Redis, Memcached)

Caching is one of the most effective ways to improve the performance of a web application by reducing the time spent on repetitive and costly operations (such as database queries or file reads). There are various caching strategies you can use in PHP applications.

1. **File Caching**:

o **What is File Caching?**: File caching involves storing computed data or query results in files on the server's filesystem. When the same request is made again, the application retrieves the data from the file instead of regenerating it or querying the database.

o **Implementation**: PHP provides simple ways to implement file caching by using `file_put_contents()` to save data and `file_get_contents()` to retrieve data from cached files.

Example: File Caching:

php

```php
<?php
$cacheFile = 'cache/data.cache';
$cacheTime = 3600;   // Cache lifetime in
seconds

if (file_exists($cacheFile) && time() -
filemtime($cacheFile) < $cacheTime) {
    // Read from cache
    $data = file_get_contents($cacheFile);
} else {
    // Generate data (e.g., from a database
query)
```

```
$data = 'Fresh Data: ' . date("Y-m-d
H:i:s");

// Save to cache
file_put_contents($cacheFile, $data);
}

echo $data;
?>
```

2. **Redis**:

   o **What is Redis?**: Redis is an in-memory data
      structure store that is commonly used as a caching
      solution for PHP web applications. It allows for
      very fast data retrieval and supports complex data
      types like strings, hashes, lists, and sets.

   o **Installing Redis for PHP**:

   ▪ Install Redis on your server:

```
bash
```

```
sudo  apt-get  install  redis-
server
```

   ▪ Install the PHP Redis extension:

```
bash
```

```
pecl install redis
```

281

3. **Example: Using Redis for Caching**:

4. php

5.

6. <?php

7. $redis = new Redis();

8. $redis->connect('127.0.0.1', 6379);

9.

10. $cacheKey = 'user_data';

11. $cacheTime = 3600;   // Cache time in seconds

12.

13. if ($redis->exists($cacheKey)) {

14.   // Fetch from cache

15. $data = $redis->get($cacheKey);

16. } else {

17.   // Generate data (e.g., from database)

18. $data = 'Fresh Data: ' . date("Y-m-d H:i:s");

19.

20.   // Save to Redis cache

21. $redis->setex($cacheKey, $cacheTime, $data);

22. }

23.

24. echo $data;

25. ?>

o Redis provides high-speed data access and is suitable for scenarios where fast read and write operations are critical.

26. **Memcached**:

   o **What is Memcached?**: Memcached is another in-memory caching system that is used for speeding up dynamic web applications by caching data in RAM.

   o **Installing Memcached for PHP**:

      ▪ Install Memcached on your server:

      bash

      sudo apt-get install memcached

      ▪ Install the Memcached PHP extension:

      bash

      pecl install memcached

27. **Example: Using Memcached for Caching**:

```
28.  php
29.
30.  <?php
31.  $memcached = new Memcached();
32.  $memcached->addServer('127.0.0.1',
     11211);
33.
```

```
34. $cacheKey = 'product_data';
35. $cacheTime = 3600;  // Cache lifetime in
    seconds
36.
37. $data = $memcached->get($cacheKey);
38. if ($data === false) {
39.     // Generate data (e.g., from
    database)
40.     $data = 'Fresh Data: ' . date("Y-m-d
    H:i:s");
41.
42.     // Save to Memcached
43.     $memcached->set($cacheKey, $data,
    $cacheTime);
44. }
45.
46. echo $data;
47. ?>
```

  o Memcached is well-suited for scenarios where
     multiple servers need to access shared cached
     data, making it ideal for large-scale distributed
     applications.

Optimizing MySQL Queries and Database Performance

MySQL is the most widely used database system in PHP
applications. Optimizing MySQL queries and database

284

interactions can significantly improve the performance of your application.

1. **Optimizing SQL Queries**:
   o **Avoiding SELECT ***: Always specify the columns you need rather than using SELECT *. This reduces the amount of data transferred from the database and speeds up the query.

   Example:

   ```sql
   SELECT name, email FROM users WHERE active = 1;
   ```

   o **Using WHERE Clauses Efficiently**: Ensure that your WHERE clauses use indexed columns to speed up query execution.
   o **Using JOIN Properly**: Instead of querying multiple tables separately, use JOIN to fetch related data in a single query.

   Example: Optimizing JOIN:

   ```sql
   SELECT u.name, p.title
   FROM users u
   ```

```
INNER JOIN posts p ON u.id = p.user_id
WHERE u.active = 1;
```

2. **Indexing**:
   o **What is an Index?**: An index is a data structure that improves the speed of data retrieval operations on a database table. Indexes are particularly useful for large datasets.
   o **Creating Indexes**:

   sql

   ```sql
   CREATE INDEX idx_users_name ON users (name);
   ```

3. **Database Caching**:
   o Utilize **query caching** in MySQL to store the results of frequently executed queries, reducing the need to execute the same query repeatedly.

4. **Optimizing Schema**:
   o Normalize your database to avoid redundancy and ensure data integrity. However, also consider denormalization for read-heavy applications where performance is critical.

286

Code Minification and Image Optimization

Minification and **image optimization** are essential steps in optimizing the front-end performance of your PHP application.

1. **Minifying CSS and JavaScript**:
   - o Minification removes unnecessary whitespace, comments, and formatting from CSS and JavaScript files to reduce their size and improve load times.
   - o Use tools like **UglifyJS** (for JavaScript) and **CSSNano** (for CSS) to minify files.

   Example: Minifying CSS:

   - o Use a tool like **CSSMinifier** or a build tool like **Webpack** to minify your CSS.

   Example: Minifying JavaScript:

   - o Use **UglifyJS**:

   bash

   ```
   uglifyjs app.js -o app.min.js
   ```

2. **Image Optimization**:
   - o **Image optimization** reduces the size of image files without sacrificing quality. This helps

287

reduce page load times, especially on image-heavy pages.

o   Use tools like **ImageOptim** (for Mac), **TinyPNG**, or **Imagemagick** to optimize images.

o   **Example: Using PHP for Image Compression**:

php

```php
<?php
$image = imagecreatefromjpeg('image.jpg');
imagejpeg($image, 'optimized_image.jpg',
75); // Save the image with 75% quality
imagedestroy($image);
?>
```

Summary

By the end of this chapter, you should be able to:

*   Profile your PHP applications to find performance bottlenecks using tools like **Xdebug** and **Blackfire**.
*   Implement effective **caching strategies** using **file caching**, **Redis**, and **Memcached** to speed up your application.
*   Optimize **MySQL queries** and database performance through proper indexing and query structure.

288

- Minify **CSS** and **JavaScript** files and optimize **images** to reduce load times and improve user experience.

Optimizing the performance of your PHP application is essential for scalability and user satisfaction. By using the strategies and techniques discussed in this chapter, you can ensure that your application runs efficiently, even as it grows.

CHAPTER 24

BUILDING RESTFUL APIS WITH PHP

Principles of REST Architecture

REST (Representational State Transfer) is an architectural style used for building web services. A **RESTful API** is an API that adheres to the principles of REST. REST APIs are designed to be lightweight, stateless, and use standard HTTP methods (GET, POST, PUT, DELETE) to interact with resources.

1. **Core Principles of REST**:
   o **Statelessness**: Every HTTP request from a client to the server must contain all the information needed to understand the request. The server should not store any information about the client session between requests.
   o **Uniform Interface**: REST APIs use a consistent and standardized set of conventions for communication. This simplifies the interaction between clients and servers.
   o **Resource Identification**: Resources (such as users, posts, products) are identified using URLs. Each resource has a unique URL.

290

- o **HTTP Methods**: REST uses standard HTTP methods to interact with resources:
    - **GET**: Retrieve data from the server.
    - **POST**: Create new resources.
    - **PUT**: Update existing resources.
    - **DELETE**: Delete resources.
- o **Representation of Resources**: Resources can be represented in various formats (e.g., JSON, XML). JSON is the most common format used for RESTful APIs.

2. **RESTful URL Conventions**:
    - o Use nouns to represent resources and make the URLs descriptive. For example:
        - `/users`: Retrieve all users.
        - `/users/{id}`: Retrieve a specific user by ID.
        - `/posts`: Retrieve all posts.
        - `/posts/{id}`: Retrieve a specific post by ID.
        - `/posts/{id}/comments`: Retrieve comments for a specific post.

3. **Stateless Communication**:
    - o Each request from the client should contain all the information needed to process the request. This includes authentication data, request parameters, and the resource being requested.

291

Creating a RESTful API with PHP and MySQL

Creating a RESTful API in PHP involves setting up routes for various HTTP methods and interacting with a MySQL database. In this section, we will walk through creating a basic **RESTful API** for managing a collection of **posts** using PHP and MySQL.

1. **Setting Up the Database**: First, create a database and a table for storing the posts.

   SQL Schema:

   ```sql
   CREATE DATABASE api_db;

   USE api_db;

   CREATE TABLE posts (
       id INT AUTO_INCREMENT PRIMARY KEY,
       title VARCHAR(255) NOT NULL,
       content TEXT NOT NULL,
       created_at    TIMESTAMP    DEFAULT
   CURRENT_TIMESTAMP
   );
   ```

   o   The `posts` table will store the title, content, and timestamp of each post.

2. **Creating the API**: For simplicity, we will create a simple API with routes to **GET**, **POST**, **PUT**, and **DELETE** posts.

   o **Directory Structure**:

```bash
/api
    /controllers
        PostController.php
    /models
        PostModel.php
    /public
        index.php
    /config
        config.php
```

3. **index.php (Main Entry Point)**:
4. php
5.
6. `<?php`
7. `// Include necessary files`
8. `require_once '../config/config.php';`
9. `require_once`
   `'../controllers/PostController.php';`
10.
11. `// Routing logic (simple example)`
12. `if ($_SERVER['REQUEST_METHOD'] === 'GET')`
    `{`

293

```
13.      if (isset($_GET['id'])) {
14.          $controller          =          new
   PostController();
15.          $controller-
   >getPost($_GET['id']);
16.      } else {
17.          $controller          =          new
   PostController();
18.          $controller->getAllPosts();
19.      }
20. } elseif ($_SERVER['REQUEST_METHOD'] ===
   'POST') {
21.      $controller = new PostController();
22.      $controller->createPost();
23. } elseif ($_SERVER['REQUEST_METHOD'] ===
   'PUT') {
24.      $controller = new PostController();
25.      $controller-
   >updatePost($_GET['id']);
26. } elseif ($_SERVER['REQUEST_METHOD'] ===
   'DELETE') {
27.      $controller = new PostController();
28.      $controller-
   >deletePost($_GET['id']);
29. }
30. ?>
```

- o The index.php file is the entry point for all API requests. It checks the HTTP method (GET, POST,

294

PUT, DELETE) and calls the appropriate controller method.

31. **PostController.php (Controller)**: The controller handles the request, interacts with the model, and returns the response.

Example: PostController.php:

php

```php
<?php
require_once '../models/PostModel.php';

class PostController {
    public function getAllPosts() {
        $postModel = new PostModel();
        $posts = $postModel->getAll();
        echo json_encode($posts);
    }

    public function getPost($id) {
        $postModel = new PostModel();
        $post = $postModel->get($id);
        echo json_encode($post);
    }

    public function createPost() {
```

```php
        $data                                =
json_decode(file_get_contents('php://inpu
t'), true);
        $postModel = new PostModel();
        $postModel-
>create($data['title'], $data['content']);
        echo   json_encode(["message"   =>
"Post created"]);
    }


    public function updatePost($id) {
        $data                                =
json_decode(file_get_contents('php://inpu
t'), true);
        $postModel = new PostModel();
        $postModel->update($id,
$data['title'], $data['content']);
        echo   json_encode(["message"   =>
"Post updated"]);
    }


    public function deletePost($id) {
        $postModel = new PostModel();
        $postModel->delete($id);
        echo   json_encode(["message"   =>
"Post deleted"]);
    }
}
```

- o This controller defines methods for **retrieving**, **creating**, **updating**, and **deleting** posts. It uses the `PostModel` to interact with the database.

32. **PostModel.php (Model)**: The model contains the logic for interacting with the database.

Example: PostModel.php:

php

```php
<?php
class PostModel {
    private $db;

    public function __construct() {
        $this->db            =            new
mysqli('localhost', 'root', '', 'api_db');
    }

    public function getAll() {
        $result = $this->db->query('SELECT
* FROM posts');
        return                 $result-
>fetch_all(MYSQLI_ASSOC);
    }

    public function get($id) {
        $stmt = $this->db->prepare('SELECT
* FROM posts WHERE id = ?');
```

297

```
        $stmt->bind_param('i', $id);
        $stmt->execute();
        return        $stmt->get_result()-
>fetch_assoc();
    }


    public      function      create($title,
$content) {
        $stmt = $this->db->prepare('INSERT
INTO  posts  (title,  content)  VALUES  (?,
?)');
        $stmt->bind_param('ss',      $title,
$content);
        $stmt->execute();
    }


    public   function   update($id,   $title,
$content) {
        $stmt = $this->db->prepare('UPDATE
posts SET title = ?, content = ? WHERE id
= ?');
        $stmt->bind_param('ssi',      $title,
$content, $id);
        $stmt->execute();
    }


    public function delete($id) {
        $stmt = $this->db->prepare('DELETE
FROM posts WHERE id = ?');
```

```
$stmt->bind_param('i', $id);
$stmt->execute();
    }
}
```

o The `PostModel` interacts with the `posts` table in the database to perform CRUD (Create, Read, Update, Delete) operations.

Handling JSON Data in PHP

JSON (JavaScript Object Notation) is the most common format for sending and receiving data in RESTful APIs. PHP provides several built-in functions to work with JSON data, such as `json_encode()` and `json_decode()`.

1. **Encoding Data to JSON**:
   o **json_encode()** is used to convert PHP arrays or objects into JSON format.

   Example:

   php

```
$data = ["name" => "John", "age" => 30];
echo json_encode($data);    // Outputs:
{"name":"John","age":30}
```

2. **Decoding JSON Data**:
   - ○ `json_decode()` is used to convert JSON data into a PHP array or object.

Example:

php

```
$json = '{"name":"John", "age":30}';
$data = json_decode($json, true);    //
Convert to associative array
echo $data['name'];  // Outputs: John
```

   - ○ In the context of the API, `json_decode()` is used to parse the incoming JSON data from client requests, while `json_encode()` is used to return JSON responses.

API Authentication (OAuth2, JWT)

When building APIs, it's important to secure them using authentication mechanisms. Two common approaches to API authentication are **OAuth2** and **JWT (JSON Web Tokens)**.

1. **OAuth2**:
   - ○ **OAuth2** is an authorization framework that allows third-party applications to access user data

without exposing credentials. It is widely used by services like Google, Facebook, and GitHub.

- o OAuth2 involves obtaining an access token, which is used in API requests to authenticate and authorize the user.

2. **JWT (JSON Web Tokens)**:

- o **JWT** is a compact, URL-safe token format used for securely transmitting information between parties. It is commonly used for user authentication in modern web applications.

- o A JWT consists of three parts: the **header**, the **payload**, and the **signature**. The server generates the JWT after authenticating the user and includes it in the response. The client sends this token in subsequent requests for authentication.

Example: Generating a JWT in PHP:

php

```php
<?php
$header = base64_encode(json_encode(['alg'
=> 'HS256', 'typ' => 'JWT']));
$payload                                =
base64_encode(json_encode(['user_id'    =>
123, 'exp' => time() + 3600]));
```

```php
$signature                              =
base64_encode(hash_hmac('sha256', $header
. '.' . $payload, 'secret', true));

$jwt = $header . '.' . $payload . '.' .
$signature;
echo $jwt;
```

Example: Verifying a JWT:

php

```php
<?php
list($header, $payload, $signature)     =
explode('.', $jwt);

$validSignature     =      hash_hmac('sha256',
$header . '.' . $payload, 'secret', true);
if              ($validSignature              ===
base64_decode($signature)) {
    echo "Valid token!";
} else {
    echo "Invalid token!";
}
```

- o The token can then be included in the Authorization header of API requests like so:

    makefile

```
Authorization: Bearer <token>
```

Summary

By the end of this chapter, you should be able to:

- Understand the core principles of **REST architecture** and how to design a **RESTful API**.
- Create a basic **RESTful API** in PHP and MySQL that supports **CRUD operations** (Create, Read, Update, Delete).
- Handle **JSON data** in PHP using `json_encode()` and `json_decode()`.
- Implement **API authentication** using standards like **OAuth2** and **JWT** to secure your API endpoints.

Building RESTful APIs in PHP is essential for creating dynamic and interactive web applications. By following best practices for API design and security, you can create scalable and secure APIs that integrate smoothly with your applications.

CHAPTER 25

PHP AND CONTENT MANAGEMENT SYSTEMS (CMS)

Introduction to CMS (e.g., WordPress, Joomla, Drupal)

A **Content Management System (CMS)** is a web application designed to simplify the creation, management, and modification of digital content. It allows non-technical users to manage their website's content without needing to understand code or web development. CMS platforms are widely used for websites, blogs, e-commerce stores, and more. In this chapter, we'll look at some of the most popular PHP-based CMS platforms: **WordPress**, **Joomla**, and **Drupal**.

1. **WordPress**:
   o **WordPress** is the most popular CMS in the world, powering over 40% of websites on the internet. It is open-source and has a large community of developers and users.
   o **Key Features**:
      ▪ Easy to use, even for beginners.
      ▪ Highly customizable with thousands of themes and plugins.

304

- Large community and extensive documentation.
- Supports blog posts, pages, multimedia, and custom content types.

Example Use Case: WordPress is perfect for blogs, business websites, and personal projects. It is scalable and can be extended with plugins for SEO, security, social sharing, and e-commerce.

2. **Joomla**:

   o **Joomla** is a versatile CMS that sits between WordPress and Drupal in terms of complexity. It is suitable for building more complex websites, like online communities or e-commerce sites.

   o **Key Features**:

      - Supports custom content types and flexibility in content display.
      - Has a powerful menu system and multilingual support.
      - A bit more technical than WordPress but still user-friendly for site administrators.

Example Use Case: Joomla is often used for community-based websites, educational platforms, or websites requiring complex content structures.

3. **Drupal**:

  o **Drupal** is a highly flexible and customizable CMS aimed at developers. It provides the most control over how content is structured and displayed, making it suitable for building complex websites.

  o **Key Features**:
    - Highly flexible and scalable, ideal for large, data-heavy websites.
    - Custom content types, fields, and relationships are powerful features.
    - Can be more challenging for non-developers but provides complete control for developers.

  Example Use Case: Drupal is ideal for large-scale websites like government portals, university websites, or complex e-commerce platforms.

Customizing and Extending a PHP-Based CMS

One of the strengths of CMS platforms like WordPress, Joomla, and Drupal is their **extensibility**. You can extend their functionality with custom themes and plugins. Here's an overview of how you can customize and extend a PHP-based CMS:

1. **Customizing Themes**: Themes control the appearance of a website. Most CMS platforms provide pre-designed themes, but you can customize them or create your own. Themes consist of templates (HTML structure), styles (CSS), and assets (images, fonts, etc.).

   o **WordPress Theme Customization**:

      ▪ WordPress themes are typically built using **PHP**, **HTML**, **CSS**, and **JavaScript**. You can customize an existing theme or build one from scratch.

      ▪ Themes are stored in the /wp-content/themes/ directory, and you can create child themes to preserve your customizations even when the parent theme is updated.

   Example: Customizing a WordPress Theme:

   php

```php
<?php
// This is a basic example of a WordPress
theme header
?>
<!DOCTYPE html>
<html <?php language_attributes(); ?>>
<head>
```

307

```
    <meta    charset="<?php    bloginfo(
'charset' ); ?>">
    <title><?php   bloginfo(  'name'  );
?></title>
    <?php wp_head(); ?>
</head>
<body <?php body_class(); ?>>
    <header>
        <h1><a  href="<?php  echo  esc_url(
home_url( '/' ) ); ?>"><?php bloginfo(
'name' ); ?></a></h1>
        <nav><?php wp_nav_menu(); ?></nav>
    </header>
```

2. **Creating Plugins**: Plugins extend the functionality of a CMS by adding new features or modifying existing ones. A plugin can add anything from simple functionality (like a contact form) to complex systems (like e-commerce).

    o **WordPress Plugin Example**:

        ▪ WordPress plugins are typically located in the `/wp-content/plugins/` directory.

        ▪ You can create a plugin by simply creating a PHP file and adding functionality.

    Example: Basic WordPress Plugin:

    php

```php
<?php
/*
Plugin Name: My Custom Plugin
Description: Adds a custom greeting to the
website.
Version: 1.0
*/

function my_custom_greeting() {
    return   "<p>Hello,   welcome   to   my
site!</p>";
}

add_shortcode(                  'greeting',
'my_custom_greeting' );
?>
```

- o This plugin defines a shortcode ([greeting])
  that can be placed on any page or post, which
  displays a custom greeting.

Building a Simple CMS from Scratch with PHP

Building a custom CMS from scratch involves several key components: content management, database interactions, user authentication, and an admin panel. In this section, we will outline how to build a simple CMS with PHP.

309

1. **Project Setup**: First, we need to create a database schema to store our content and user information.

   Database Schema:

   ```sql
   sql

   CREATE DATABASE simple_cms;

   USE simple_cms;

   CREATE TABLE posts (
       id INT AUTO_INCREMENT PRIMARY KEY,
       title VARCHAR(255) NOT NULL,
       content TEXT NOT NULL,
       created_at       TIMESTAMP       DEFAULT
   CURRENT_TIMESTAMP
   );

   CREATE TABLE users (
       id INT AUTO_INCREMENT PRIMARY KEY,
       username VARCHAR(50) NOT NULL,
       password VARCHAR(255) NOT NULL
   );
   ```

2. **Building the CMS**: We will create three parts: **Frontend**, **Admin Panel**, and **Database Interaction**.
   - **Frontend (Displaying Posts)**: The frontend will display the posts stored in the database.

310

Example: Display Posts (index.php):

php

```php
<?php
// Include database connection
include('db.php');

// Fetch all posts
$query = "SELECT * FROM posts ORDER
BY created_at DESC";
$result     =     mysqli_query($conn,
$query);
while           ($post           =
mysqli_fetch_assoc($result)) {
    echo  "<h2>"  .  $post['title']  .
"</h2>";
    echo  "<p>"  .  $post['content']  .
"</p>";
}
?>
```

○ **Admin Panel (Managing Posts)**: The admin
   panel allows users to add, edit, and delete posts.
   We'll use simple forms to handle post creation
   and updates.

Example: Admin Panel (admin.php):

311

php

```php
<?php
// Admin authentication
session_start();
if (!isset($_SESSION['username'])) {
    header('Location: login.php');
    exit();
}

// Include database connection
include('db.php');

// Insert new post
if ($_SERVER['REQUEST_METHOD'] ==
'POST') {
    $title = $_POST['title'];
    $content = $_POST['content'];
    $query = "INSERT INTO posts
(title, content) VALUES ('$title',
'$content')";
    mysqli_query($conn, $query);
}

?>
<h2>Add New Post</h2>
<form method="POST">
    <label>Title:</label><br>
```

```
        <input                type="text"
name="title"><br><br>
        <label>Content:</label><br>
        <textarea
name="content"></textarea><br><br>
        <button         type="submit">Save
Post</button>
    </form>
```

3. **User Authentication**: Add a simple login system to authenticate users before they can access the admin panel.

Example: Login (login.php):

```
php

<?php
session_start();
include('db.php');

if ($_SERVER['REQUEST_METHOD'] == 'POST')
{
    $username = $_POST['username'];
    $password = $_POST['password'];

    $query = "SELECT * FROM users WHERE
username = '$username'";
    $result = mysqli_query($conn, $query);
    $user = mysqli_fetch_assoc($result);
```

313

```
    if                ($user            &&
password_verify($password,
$user['password'])) {
        $_SESSION['username'] = $username;
        header('Location: admin.php');
    } else {
        echo    "Invalid    username    or
password.";
    }
}
?>
<form method="POST">
    <label>Username:</label><br>
    <input                    type="text"
name="username"><br><br>
    <label>Password:</label><br>
    <input                type="password"
name="password"><br><br>
    <button type="submit">Login</button>
</form>
```

Integrating PHP with Themes and Plugins

Most CMS platforms, like WordPress, offer extensibility through **themes** and **plugins**. In this section, we'll outline how you can integrate your PHP-based CMS with custom themes and plugins.

1. **Themes**:

- o A **theme** controls the visual appearance of a website. Themes often consist of HTML templates, CSS, and JavaScript files.
- o You can integrate themes into your CMS by creating a **theme folder** and referencing the relevant theme files (e.g., `header.php`, `footer.php`) in your templates.

Example: Integrating a Theme:

php

```php
<?php include('themes/header.php'); ?>
<div class="content">
    <?php echo $post['content']; ?>
</div>
<?php include('themes/footer.php'); ?>
```

2. **Plugins**:

- o **Plugins** extend the functionality of the CMS by adding new features. A plugin can add anything from custom widgets to additional content management functionality.
- o To integrate plugins, you can create a plugin directory and load plugin files into the CMS dynamically.

Example: Simple Plugin:

315

```php
php

// In plugins/hello_world.php
function hello_world() {
    echo "<h2>Hello, World!</h2>";
}

// In your main CMS file
include('plugins/hello_world.php');
hello_world();
```

Summary

By the end of this chapter, you should be able to:

- Understand the **principles of REST architecture** and how CMS platforms like **WordPress, Joomla**, and **Drupal** are built.
- **Customize** and extend a PHP-based CMS by building custom themes and plugins.
- **Build a simple CMS from scratch** using PHP and MySQL for managing content and user authentication.
- **Integrate themes and plugins** to customize the appearance and functionality of your CMS.

Building a CMS with PHP can be a powerful way to create custom content management solutions. With the right combination of

PHP, MySQL, and extensibility features like themes and plugins, you can create highly flexible and scalable CMS platforms.

CHAPTER 26

BEST PRACTICES AND CODE QUALITY IN PHP

Writing Clean and Maintainable Code

Writing clean, readable, and maintainable code is essential for any PHP developer, especially as projects grow larger and more complex. Clean code is easier to understand, modify, and extend, making it more maintainable in the long term.

1. **Use Meaningful Variable and Function Names**:
   o Always use **descriptive names** for variables, functions, and classes. The names should convey the purpose of the entity, making the code easier to understand.
   o Avoid abbreviations unless they are widely accepted (e.g., $db for database).

Example:

```php
php

// Bad naming
$a = "John";
$b = "Doe";
```

```
$c = $a . " " . $b;

// Good naming
$firstName = "John";
$lastName = "Doe";
$fullName = $firstName . " " . $lastName;
```

2. **Keep Functions and Methods Small**:

   o   A function should perform a single task and be small enough that it can be easily understood. If a function is too large or does too many things, break it down into smaller, more manageable functions.

Example:

php

```
// Bad function
function processData($data) {
    // process data
    // validate data
    // save to database
    // send email
}

// Good function
function validateData($data) { ... }
function saveData($data) { ... }
```

```php
function sendEmail($email) { ... }
```

3. **Follow Consistent Code Formatting**:
   - Consistent formatting (e.g., indentation, spacing, and braces placement) improves readability. Use **tabs or spaces** consistently (the standard is 4 spaces for indentation in PHP).
   - Stick to a style guide and apply it across the project.

Example:

php

```php
// Consistent formatting
if ($condition) {
    echo "Hello";
}
```

4. **Avoid Duplication (DRY Principle)**:
   - **Don't Repeat Yourself**. Repeated code should be extracted into functions or classes. Duplicating logic makes maintenance difficult and increases the chances of introducing errors.

Example:

php

```php
// Bad: Repeated logic
if ($userType == 'admin') {
    echo "Welcome admin";
} elseif ($userType == 'manager') {
    echo "Welcome manager";
}


// Good: Avoid repetition by using a
function
function greetUser($userType) {
    return "Welcome $userType";
}
echo greetUser($userType);
```

Code Reviews and Collaborative Development

Code reviews are a critical part of collaborative development. They help ensure that code is clean, functional, and adheres to best practices. Code reviews also promote knowledge sharing and improve code quality across a team.

1. **The Importance of Code Reviews**:
    - **Quality Assurance**: Code reviews help catch bugs, security vulnerabilities, and issues that might otherwise go unnoticed.
    - **Knowledge Sharing**: Through code reviews, developers share their knowledge and techniques, improving the entire team's skillset.

- o **Consistency**: Code reviews ensure that all code follows consistent standards and patterns, making the project easier to maintain.

2. **Best Practices for Code Reviews**:
   - o **Keep Reviews Small**: Reviewing too many lines of code at once can lead to fatigue and missed issues. Aim for small, focused code reviews (around 200–400 lines at a time).
   - o **Be Constructive**: Provide feedback that is clear and respectful. Point out issues and suggest solutions without being overly critical.
   - o **Focus on Functionality and Style**: Check if the code works as expected, and also ensure that it follows coding standards (e.g., naming conventions, formatting).
   - o **Automated Tests**: Make sure the code passes all tests before the review. Encourage developers to write unit tests for their code.

Following PHP-FIG Standards (PSR)

The **PHP Framework Interop Group (PHP-FIG)** defines a set of standards for PHP development that help ensure consistency across PHP projects. The most widely adopted standards are the **PSR (PHP Standards Recommendations)**, which help developers write code that is compatible with various libraries, frameworks, and tools.

1. **PSR-1: Basic Coding Standard**:
   o PSR-1 defines basic coding conventions such as using **UTF-8 encoding** and ensuring that class names follow the **PSR-4** autoloading standard.
   o It also recommends that files should have a **single class** or **interface**.

2. **PSR-2: Coding Style Guide**:
   o PSR-2 is a detailed coding style guide that covers the formatting of PHP code. Some of its key rules include:
     - **Indentation**: Use 4 spaces per indentation level.
     - **Line Length**: Lines should not exceed 120 characters.
     - **Braces**: Opening braces for classes, functions, and control structures must be on the same line as the declaration.

   Example (PSR-2):

```php
php

<?php

class MyClass
```

```
{
    public function myMethod()
    {
        if ($condition) {
            // do something
        }
    }
}
```

3. **PSR-4: Autoloader Standard**:
   - o PSR-4 specifies how to autoload PHP classes using namespaces. It ensures that class names and file paths follow a consistent structure.
   - o The **namespace** should correspond to the file path, and each class should be in its own file.

Example (PSR-4):

   - o The `\MyNamespace\MyClass` class should be located at `src/MyNamespace/MyClass.php`.

4. **PSR-12: Extended Coding Style Guide**:
   - o PSR-12 extends PSR-2 by providing additional details about docblocks, control structures, and class declarations.
   - o It includes rules for **function arguments**, **visibility keywords**, and **PHPDoc annotations** for better documentation.

324

Documenting Your Code and Using Comments Effectively

Commenting your code is essential for ensuring that others (or you in the future) can understand the logic behind your code. Well-documented code improves maintainability and reduces the time needed for future debugging and enhancements.

1. **Types of Comments**:
    - **Inline Comments**: Used to explain individual lines or short blocks of code.
    - **Block Comments**: Used to explain a section of code or complex logic in detail.
    - **PHPDoc Comments**: Used to describe classes, methods, and functions. These comments can be used by IDEs for autocompletion and can generate documentation.

2. **Inline Comments**:
    - Keep inline comments concise and to the point. They should explain "why" something is done, not "what" is done (the code itself should make the "what" clear).

Example:

php

```
// Calculate the total price with tax
```

325

```
$totalPrice = $price + ($price * $taxRate);
```

3. **Block Comments**:
   - o   Use block comments for explaining sections of code or the rationale behind complex logic.

Example:

```php
php

/*
 * This section of the code handles user
input validation
 * to ensure that only valid email
addresses are submitted.
 */
if                 (!filter_var($email,
FILTER_VALIDATE_EMAIL)) {
    echo "Invalid email format";
}
```

4. **PHPDoc Comments**:
   - o   **PHPDoc** comments provide detailed descriptions of classes, methods, functions, and parameters. These comments can be parsed by tools like **phpDocumentor** to generate documentation automatically.

Example (PHPDoc):

```php
php

/**
 * Calculates the area of a rectangle.
 *
 * @param float $width The width of the
rectangle.
 * @param float $height The height of the
rectangle.
 * @return float The area of the rectangle.
 */
function calculateArea($width, $height) {
    return $width * $height;
}
```

- o **Explanation**:
  - **@param**: Describes the parameters the function expects.
  - **@return**: Describes what the function returns.

Summary

By the end of this chapter, you should be able to:

- Write **clean, readable, and maintainable** PHP code by using meaningful names, keeping functions small, and following consistent formatting.
- Understand the importance of **code reviews** and the best practices for conducting them, fostering collaborative development.
- Follow **PHP-FIG standards (PSR)**, including PSR-1, PSR-2, PSR-4, and PSR-12, to ensure your code adheres to established conventions.
- Use **comments** effectively to document your code, making it easier for others to understand and maintain.

Writing clean code, following best practices, and maintaining high code quality are crucial aspects of professional PHP development. By adhering to these practices, you ensure that your code is easy to read, scalable, and maintainable, leading to better collaboration and fewer issues down the road.

CHAPTER 27

THE FUTURE OF PHP AND WEB DEVELOPMENT

Trends and Innovations in PHP Development (PHP 8, New Features)

PHP has come a long way since its inception, and the latest versions, particularly **PHP 8**, introduce significant improvements in performance, functionality, and developer experience. In this section, we'll explore the new features of PHP 8 and how they impact modern PHP development.

1. **PHP 8 Features**:

   o **Just-in-Time (JIT) Compiler**: One of the most significant performance improvements in PHP 8 is the addition of the **JIT compiler**. JIT allows PHP to compile parts of the code into machine code at runtime, resulting in faster execution, especially for CPU-intensive tasks. However, for typical web applications, the performance gains are most noticeable in computation-heavy operations (e.g., data processing or image manipulation).

329

o **Named Arguments**: Named arguments allow you to pass arguments to a function by specifying the parameter names, making code more readable and reducing the chance of making mistakes when passing arguments in a different order.

Example:

php

```php
function createUser($name, $email, $role) {
    // function logic
}

// PHP 8 named arguments
createUser(name: 'John', role: 'Admin', email: 'john@example.com');
```

o **Union Types**: PHP 8 introduces **union types**, allowing a parameter or return type to accept multiple types, enhancing type safety and flexibility.

Example:

php

```
function add(int|float $a, int|float
$b): int|float {
    return $a + $b;
}
```

o **Attributes (Annotations)**: PHP 8 introduces **attributes** (also known as annotations) to replace docblock-based annotations. Attributes allow you to add metadata to classes, methods, and properties, making it easier to read and process the metadata programmatically.

Example:

```
php

#[Route('/home')]
class HomeController {
    // controller code
}
```

o **Match Expressions**: PHP 8 introduces **match expressions**, which are similar to switch statements but with more flexibility and strict type comparisons. This provides a cleaner way to handle multiple conditions.

Example:

```php
php

$result = match ($status) {
    'pending' => 'Order is pending',
    'shipped' => 'Order has been
shipped',
    'delivered' => 'Order has been
delivered',
    default => 'Unknown status',
};
```

2. **Performance Improvements**:
   o **PHP 8** has shown impressive **performance improvements** over previous versions, particularly due to the JIT compiler and various internal optimizations. As PHP continues to evolve, future versions will likely include further performance enhancements, making PHP a more viable option for performance-critical applications.

3. **Deprecations and Future Changes**:
   o PHP 8 also marks the **deprecation** of certain features, such as the `create_function()` and the `each()` function, which are being phased out. This trend will continue in future versions as PHP evolves to remove outdated functionality in favor of more modern solutions.

PHP's Role in Modern Web Development (Microservices, Serverless)

PHP continues to play a central role in modern web development, despite the rise of other programming languages like JavaScript and Python. PHP is still one of the most widely used languages for web development, and it is adapting to new trends like **microservices** and **serverless architectures**.

1. **Microservices Architecture**:
   - **Microservices** is an architectural style that structures an application as a collection of loosely coupled, independently deployable services. PHP is becoming more and more suitable for microservices, as its performance and scalability improve.
   - **PHP and Microservices**:
     - **Frameworks like Laravel and Symfony** provide robust solutions for building microservices. Laravel, for example, comes with tools for API creation, queue management, and task scheduling, making it easier to build microservices.
     - Microservices can communicate with each other through **RESTful APIs** or **message brokers** (such as RabbitMQ or

333

Kafka). PHP is well-equipped to handle REST APIs with frameworks like Laravel, which simplifies API development.

Example of Microservices in PHP:

- o In a PHP-based microservice architecture, each service could be a separate Laravel application, communicating with others using HTTP or queues.
- o A microservice might handle authentication, another service might manage user profiles, and yet another might handle payments. Each of these services can scale independently, allowing developers to build highly flexible and scalable applications.

2. **Serverless Architectures**:
   - o **Serverless** computing allows developers to run applications without managing servers. Instead of provisioning and maintaining servers, you can deploy individual functions that automatically scale in response to demand. This is ideal for event-driven applications, where functions are triggered by specific events (such as HTTP requests, database changes, or file uploads).
   - o **PHP and Serverless**:

- PHP can be used in serverless environments with services like **AWS Lambda** or **Google Cloud Functions**. With the appropriate runtime environment, you can deploy PHP functions that run only when needed, saving costs on idle server time.

- **Frameworks like Laravel Vapor** allow you to easily deploy your Laravel applications to serverless platforms like AWS Lambda, making it easier to build and scale applications in a serverless environment.

Example: Using PHP with Serverless:

o With **AWS Lambda**, you can create PHP functions to handle API requests, process files, or interact with other AWS services, all without managing infrastructure.

3. **PHP's Role in API-First Development**:

o The **API-first** approach is becoming increasingly popular for modern web applications. This means that APIs are treated as the primary means of interaction, with front-end applications (like single-page applications or mobile apps) consuming the API.

o PHP is well-suited for API-first development, thanks to tools like **Laravel** (with its built-in API support) and **Slim Framework** for lightweight API development. PHP's flexibility allows developers to build robust APIs for client-side applications.

Resources for Continuous Learning (Communities, Forums, Blogs)

To stay updated with the latest developments in PHP and web development, it's important to be an active part of the PHP community and continue learning. Here are some resources that can help you stay ahead of the curve.

1. **PHP Communities and Forums**:
   o **PHP Internals**: The official **PHP Internals** mailing list is where discussions about new features and changes to PHP occur. You can participate in the development of PHP itself and stay up to date with upcoming changes.
   o **Stack Overflow**: One of the largest communities for developers, Stack Overflow has a dedicated PHP tag where developers can ask and answer questions.
   o **Reddit (r/PHP)**: The **r/PHP** subreddit is a great place to find articles, tutorials, and news about

PHP. It's a welcoming community for developers of all skill levels.

2. **PHP Blogs**:

   o **PHP The Right Way**: This website provides a comprehensive and up-to-date guide to best practices in PHP development. It's an essential resource for PHP developers who want to follow best practices and learn new techniques.

   o **Laravel News**: If you're working with Laravel, **Laravel News** is the go-to blog for updates, tutorials, and news about the Laravel ecosystem.

   o **PHP.net Documentation**: The official **PHP documentation** (https://www.php.net/docs.php) is an invaluable resource for learning about built-in functions, libraries, and features in PHP.

   o **TutsPlus PHP Tutorials**: **TutsPlus** offers a wide range of tutorials on PHP development, including how-to guides, tutorials for beginners, and advanced topics for experienced developers.

3. **PHP Conferences and Meetups**:

   o **PHP Conference**: Attending PHP conferences is an excellent way to network with other developers, learn about the latest trends in PHP, and hear from industry experts.

   o **PHP Meetup Groups**: Local **PHP Meetup** groups allow you to connect with other PHP developers in your area. These meetups are great for learning, collaboration, and sharing experiences.

4. **YouTube Channels**:

   o **Laracasts**: Laracasts offers high-quality video tutorials on Laravel and PHP in general. It's an excellent resource for learning PHP best practices and advanced topics.

   o **PHPClasses.org**: The **PHPClasses.org YouTube channel** provides tutorials and discussions about PHP tools, libraries, and frameworks.

   o **Traversy Media**: Brad Traversy's YouTube channel includes tutorials on web development, including PHP, Laravel, and many other modern technologies.

Summary

By the end of this chapter, you should be able to:

- Understand the new features and **innovations in PHP** (PHP 8) and how they impact web development.

- Explore **PHP's role** in modern web development, including **microservices, serverless architectures**, and **API-first development**.
- Leverage **resources for continuous learning**, including **communities, forums, blogs**, and **conferences**, to stay updated with the latest PHP trends and best practices.

PHP continues to evolve and remain an essential language for web development. By keeping up with the latest innovations and continuously improving your skills, you can ensure that your PHP applications remain efficient, secure, and up to date with modern web development practices.